A World Power

Power

1934 to the Present

DEBATABLE ISSUES
IN U.S. HISTORY

VOLUME FIVE

A World
Power

1934 to the Present

GP

GREENWOOD PRESS
Westport, Connecticut - London

Library of Congress Cataloging-in-Publication Data

Debatable issues in U.S. history / by Creative Media Applications.
        p. cm.—(Middle school reference)
    Includes bibliographical references and index.
ISBN 0–313–32910–9 (set : alk. paper)—ISBN 0–313–32911–7 (v. 1 : alk. paper)—
ISBN 0–313–32912–5 (v. 2 : alk. paper)—ISBN 0–313–32913–3 (v. 3 : alk. paper)—
ISBN 0–313–32914–1 (v. 4 : alk. paper)—ISBN 0–313–32915–X (v. 5 : alk. paper)
     1. United States—History—Miscellanea—Juvenile literature.
2. United States—Politics and government—Miscellanea—Juvenile literature.
3. United States—Social conditions—Miscellanea—Juvenile literature.
4. Critical thinking—Study and teaching (Middle school)—United States.
[1. United States—History. 2. United States—Politics and
government.] I. Creative Media Applications. II. Series.
E178.3.D35   2004
973—dc22   2003056802

British Library Cataloguing in Publication Data is available.

Copyright © 2004 by Greenwood Publishing Group, Inc.

All rights reserved. No portion of this book may be reproduced, by any process or technique,
without the express written consent of the publisher.

Library of Congress Catalog Card Number: 2003056802
ISBN: 0–313–32910–9 (set)
         0–313–32911–7 (vol. 1)
         0–313–32912–5 (vol. 2)
         0–313–32913–3 (vol. 3)
         0–313–32914–1 (vol. 4)
         0–313–32925–X (vol. 5)

First published in 2004

Greenwood Press, 88 Post Road West, Westport, CT 06881
An imprint of Greenwood Publishing Group, Inc.
www.greenwood.com

Printed in the United States of America

♾™
The paper used in this book complies with the Permanent Paper Standard issued by the
National Information Standards Organization (Z39.48–1984).

10 9 8 7 6 5 4 3 2 1

A Creative Media Applications, Inc. Production
Writer: Michael Burgan
Design and Production: Fabia Wargin Design
Editor: Matt Levine
Copyeditor: Laurie Lieb
Proofreader: Betty Pessagno
Indexer: Nara Wood
Associated Press Photo Researcher: Yvette Reyes
Consultant: Mel Urofsky, Professor Emeritus of History at Virginia Commonwealth University

Photo credits:
AP/Wide World Photographs *pages* 5, 6, 15, 21, 23, 27, 28, 30, 35, 38, 44, 47, 51, 52, 59, 61,
68, 70, 73, 75, 76, 80, 84, 87, 92, 96, 99, 101, 103, 104, 107, 111, 115, 117, 121, 123, 128, 130
© Richard T. Nowitz/CORBIS *page* 8
© CORBIS *page* 11
© PictureHistory *pages* 13
© Hulton Archives/Getty Images *page* 62
© Bettmann/CORBIS *pages* 66, 90

Contents

In the 1960s, black Americans exercised their right to protest against civil injustice. The ability of all citizens to voice their opinion is a cornerstone of the American democratic system and has resulted in vast changes in the way we legislate civil freedoms.

Introduction

*W*hen people come together in a community, they face important decisions about how to run their affairs. Since everyone does not think alike, have the same feelings, or share the same interests, disagreements often arise over key issues.

In a democratic society such as the United States, public debate helps leaders decide what action to take on the most important issues. The debates might start in Congress or another branch of the government. They are often carried on in the media, and they continue in homes, in offices, and wherever concerned citizens gather.

The five volumes of *Debatable Issues in U.S. History* look at some of the most important issues that have sparked political and social debates, from colonial times to the present day. Some of the issues have been local, such as the dispute between Roger Williams and the Puritan leaders of Massachusetts. Williams struggled to introduce the idea of religious freedom in a community that wanted just one kind of religious worship. Other issues—segregation, for example—had special significance for a large group of people. African Americans, who had once been forced to live in slavery, had to endure lingering prejudice even when they received their freedom during and after the Civil War (1861–1865). Some of the most important issues have touched all Americans, as the country's leaders considered whether to go to war in times of international crisis. The 2003 war in Iraq is just the latest example of that debate.

Throughout American history, certain types of issues have appeared over and over. The details may change, but Americans continue to argue over such things as: How much power should

> How much power should the national government have?

the national government have? How does society balance personal freedom with the need to protect the common good? Which political party has the best vision for strengthening the country? Who should America choose as its friends and its enemies around the world?

> How does society balance personal freedom with the need to protect the common good?

Historians have debated the importance of certain events for hundreds of years. New facts emerge, or interpretations change as the world changes. From the historians' view, almost any issue is debatable. This series, however, focuses on the events and issues that Americans debated as they occurred. Today, few people would question whether the American colonies should have declared their independence from Great Britain; it seems almost impossible to imagine anything else happening. However, to the Americans of the day, the issue was not so clear-cut. Colonial leaders strongly disagreed on what action to take in the months before Thomas Jefferson wrote the Declaration of Independence.

Students at the University of Pennsylvania offer information about the issue of reproductive rights. The debate between the pro-choice and the pro-life movements has lasted for decades and will most likely continue indefinitely.

At times in the past, debate over key issues might have been limited. From the seventeenth century through most of the nineteenth century, transportation and communication were primitive compared with today. Still, through letters, sermons, newspapers, and government documents, opposing ideas were shared and debated. The lack of electronic communication did not weaken the passion with which people held their beliefs and their desire to shape public issues.

Today, the Internet and other forms of digital communication let millions of people debate crucial issues that face the United States. Better technology, however, does not make it easier for people to settle these issues. As *Debatable Issues in U.S. History* shows, strong emotions often fuel the discussions over the issues. At times, those emotions spill out in violence. On issues that matter most, people are often unwilling to give in, modify their views, or admit that they are wrong. Those attitudes can lead to debates that last for generations. Abortion was a heated issue in 1973, when the U.S. Supreme Court ruled that a woman could legally have an abortion if she chose. Abortion remains a divisive issue today, and there is not much chance that the debate will end.

Who should America choose as its friends and its enemies around the world?

Debates and disagreements can make it hard for governments to function smoothly. Still, debate allows Americans to explore all sides of an issue. Debate can also lead to new and better ideas that no one had considered before. U.S. Supreme Court Justice William Brennan once noted that Americans have "a profound national commitment to the principle that debate on public issues should be uninhibited, robust, and wide open." That commitment first took shape in colonial America, and it continues today.

A Note to the Reader

The quotations in Debatable Issues in U.S. History *are taken from primary sources, the writings and speeches of the people debating the important issues of their time. Some of the words, phrases, and images in these sources may be offensive by today's standards, but they are an authentic example of our past history. Also, some of the quotes have been slightly changed to reflect the modern spelling of the original words or to make the meaning of the quotes clearer. All metric conversions in this book are approximate.*

CHAPTER ONE

The Internment of Japanese Americans

WHAT

President Franklin Roosevelt orders that all Japanese Americans
be interned, or placed in guarded camps.

ISSUES

U.S. security during wartime; the constitutional rights of
Japanese American citizens

WHERE

Western United States

WHEN

1942–1946

*T*he first Japanese immigrants reached the United States during the 1860s, settling in California. Thousands also went to work on farms in Hawaii, which became a U.S. territory in 1898. Most Japanese who came to the mainland lived in California, with smaller communities springing up in other Western states, particularly Arizona, Oregon, and Washington. Many soon became successful farmers and shopkeepers. Their success, however, angered some white Americans. These people accused the Japanese of controlling the production of some fruits and vegetables and hurting their businesses.

The Japanese also faced racism. Some white Americans considered the Japanese—and other Asians—inferior to whites. The racists disliked the Japanese because most were not Christian and they came from a country that did not have a democratic government. "They are not," one California politician said in 1900, "the stuff of which American citizens can be made." The next year, a report by a government organization said that all Japanese were "tricky, unreliable, and dishonest."

Americans who disliked the Japanese favored limiting their right to own land and restricting Japanese immigration to the United States. A 1913 California law prevented immigrants who were not U.S. citizens from owning land. Many Japanese farmers got around the law by giving their land to their Nisei children. In 1924, Congress passed a law that set limits on immigration. The law ended almost all Japanese immigration to the United States.

Fast Fact

Japanese immigrants to the United States were called Issei (first generation). Their children born in the United States automatically became U.S. citizens. They were called Nisei (second generation).

Americans and World War II

On December 7, 1941, hundreds of Japanese warplanes streaked over the skies of Pearl Harbor, Hawaii. With bombs, torpedoes, and machine guns, the planes attacked the U.S. Navy base there. The surprise attack killed more than 2,000 Americans and brought the United States into World War II (1939–1945).

The Pearl Harbor attack raised American suspicions about the Japanese living in Hawaii and on the West Coast of the United States. Some military leaders and government officials worried that the Japanese Americans would betray the United States and try to help Japan win the war. They feared espionage—spying—and sabotage. To prevent these dangers, President Franklin Roosevelt issued an order that the military could declare an area a "military territory." Military officials could then force residents from their homes and prevent them from returning. Roosevelt gave this order in February 1942. A few weeks later, Congress gave federal courts the power to enforce the order.

Fast Fact

Roosevelt's order to remove people from military territories was called Executive Order 9066. "Executive" refers to the branch of the U.S. government led by the president.

Many Japanese Americans fought as American soldiers, even while their families were interned in camps. Here a Japanese American family sits in front of the flag, holding a picture of their son who is off fighting in the war for the United States.

Although Roosevelt's order did not specifically mention Japanese Americans, he and his aides wanted it applied only to them. The government soon set up a series of camps called relocation camps. About 110,000 Japanese Americans living on the West Coast, both Issei and Nisei, were interned, or forced to move into the camps. One military officer in charge of the forced removal said that anyone with even "one drop of Japanese blood...must go to the camp." The Japanese could only take whatever they could carry. Some put their remaining belongings into storage, while others sold them for less than they were worth. Some whites deceived the Japanese into thinking that they would lose everything they owned if they did not sell the goods at the cheap price.

THE OTHER ENEMIES

During World War II, the United States was also at war with Italy and Germany. Italian Americans and German Americans, however, did not face the same treatment as Japanese Americans. U.S. leaders did not consider Italians and Germans much of a threat. U.S. officials investigated some individual Italian and German aliens suspected of espionage or sabotage. The government, however, did not target U.S. citizens of Italian or German descent and did not relocate Italian or German Americans as a group, as it did with the Japanese.

Life in the Camps

The Japanese first went to temporary camps called assembly centers. Most were in California. The centers were quickly built at such places as fairgrounds, racetracks, and horse farms. One Japanese American later recalled, "There was so much horse and cow manure around…. We lived in a horse stall from May to September." After a few months at the assembly centers, the Japanese went to the internment camps, which were located in remote areas of seven states. At both the centers and the camps, armed guards looked down on the residents from towers, and barbed wire kept them inside.

Life for Japanese Americans in the internment camps was often bleak because of poor living conditions and the manual labor required to maintain even the most substandard environment. Here, men dig a drainage ditch near barracks at a relocation camp in Arkansas.

At the camps, the Japanese made their beds with pillows and mattresses stuffed with straw. In some camps, the bathrooms were unheated and the people had to walk outside to reach them. At times, the internees ate a limited diet, with few vegetables and no milk. Students attended classes within the camp, while adults worked to keep the camps running. Some internees were allowed out of the camps during the day to attend college or work on farms. Within the camps, guards had orders to shoot anyone who got too close to the fences. One internee in Arizona called his camp "a scorching Hell…beyond description and beyond tears."

In general, the internees did not question their treatment. When the relocation program began, some Japanese volunteered to leave their homes and enter the camps. They wanted to show U.S. officials that they were good citizens and would not cause trouble. Inside the camps, the leaders of the community tried to keep order. At several camps, however, the internees protested their treatment. One protest took place at Tule Lake, California, a camp for internees considered the most disloyal. In 1943, fights broke out there between some Japanese and their guards. The camp's director called in army troops and tanks, and about 350 internees were arrested.

> *Fast Fact*
>
> The U.S. government built ten relocation centers. Arizona, California, and Arkansas had two each, while Utah, Colorado, Wyoming, and Idaho each had one.

Legal Challenges to Internment

A few Japanese Americans went to court to challenge President Roosevelt's executive order and other restrictions against them. In 1942, Gordon Hirabayashi broke a curfew that required Japanese Americans to stay indoors between eight o'clock at night and six o'clock in the morning. Hirabayashi, a U.S. citizen, also refused to report to an assembly center. He was arrested on both counts and sentenced to serve three months in jail. Hirabayashi challenged his conviction, and the U.S. Supreme Court heard his case in 1943. The Court ruled that the curfew was legal and Hirabayashi should serve his sentence. The Court did not consider the other main point in the case, that under the U.S. Constitution, the relocation program was illegal.

The next year, the Supreme Court heard two more cases dealing with the internment camps. On December 18, 1944, in *Korematsu v. United States*, the Court said that the government had the constitutional right to exclude Japanese Americans from areas where they might pose a danger to security. The Court did not rule if keeping the Japanese in the camps once they left the military territories was legal. On the same day, the Court ruled on the case *Ex parte Endo*. The justices said that the government could not hold U.S. citizens in the camps if the government knew that they were loyal and did not pose a threat. The ruling meant that many Nisei would have to be freed.

President Roosevelt and his advisers learned ahead of time how the Supreme Court would rule in *Endo*. The day before the Court released its judgment, the government announced that it would free all internees except any who had publicly shown loyalty to Japan. During 1945, many Japanese Americans returned to the West Coast, and all the camps were closed by March 1946.

FIGHTING FOR AMERICA

At the beginning of World War II, the U.S. Army did not want Japanese American citizens in the military, but it eventually formed all-Japanese units that fought in Europe. The most famous, the 442nd Regimental Combat Team, was known for its bravery, and many of its members won medals for their service. About 30,000 Japanese American citizens fought for their country during the war.

After the War

The Japanese Americans who returned to their old homes sometimes found that they had lost everything they owned. Thieves had robbed warehouses and other places where the Japanese had stored their goods. The U.S. government set up a program to help repay the Japanese Americans for their losses, including property that they had sold before entering the camps. The payments, however, did not cover the true value of what they lost. One Japanese American lawyer said that "the [U.S.] Justice Department attitude was 'take it or leave it.'"

During the 1970s, several Japanese American organizations called on the U.S. government to do more for surviving internees. These efforts received a boost when researchers uncovered evidence showing that the U.S. government had broken the law during the war. In the *Korematsu* case and other trials, the government had kept some information from the judges that would have helped the Japanese Americans. The government officials also had lied about the threat that the internees posed. Federal courts threw out the convictions of Korematsu and Hirabayashi. Then, in 1988, Congress agreed to give the surviving internees $20,000 each. Presidents Ronald Reagan and George H.W. Bush also apologized for the government's actions during the war. Bush said, "We can never fully right the wrongs of the past. But we can take a clear stand for justice and recognize that serious injustices were done to Japanese Americans during World War II."

Arguments for Internment

Once Japan bombed Hawaii, many Americans had genuine fears about an attack on the West Coast, fears that seemed justified in the first few months of the war when Japan won several military victories in the Pacific. The U.S. government argued that it had the legal power to do whatever it could to protect the country during wartime—including relocating U.S. citizens. One of Roosevelt's advisers wrote a note to the president explaining what he should say about Executive Order 9066. "Authority over the movement of persons, whether citizens or non-citizens, may be exercised in time of war…. [This] is…a precautionary measure to protect the national safety." Government officials said that the order was not meant to single out any one race or group of people, though in the end, that was the result.

Several U.S. military and civilian leaders led the call to relocate Japanese Americans from the West Coast. General John DeWitt was in charge of defense for the West Coast. He claimed that he received reports that Japanese Americans were talking with officials in Japan and planning sabotage. He said that the Nisei and Issei were part of an "enemy race" and could not be trusted. California governor Culbert Olson, who supported relocation, made similar public comments.

Some California farmers admitted that they wanted the relocation for their own benefit. They wanted to take control of farmlands owned by Japanese Americans. A few people argued that the relocation would actually help the Japanese Americans. With feelings so strong against them, they would be safer in the camps, where they could be protected from any violent attacks by angry white Americans.

Once the legal challenges to relocation began, the U.S. government once again argued that Roosevelt had the power to order exclusion and relocation during wartime. In the *Korematsu* case, a majority of the U.S. Supreme Court agreed. Justice Felix Frankfurter wrote, "The Constitution does not forbid the military measures now complained of," and Justice Hugo Black said that accusing the government of racial prejudice for its actions "merely confuses the issue."

Fast Fact

In some cases, newspapers printed false reports and rumors about possible sabotage and espionage, adding to the suspicion against Japanese Americans.

In Their Own Words

Here is part of a 1942 editorial from the *San Francisco Chronicle* supporting the relocation of Japanese Americans.

[Since] the presence of enemy agents cannot be detected readily when these areas are thronged by Japanese the only course left is to remove all persons of that race for the duration of the war.

That is a clear-cut policy easily understood. Its execution should be supported by all citizens of whatever racial background...it presents an opportunity to the people of an enemy race to prove their spirit of co-operation and keep their relations with the rest of the population of this country on the firm ground of friendship.

Arguments against Internment

Before Roosevelt issued Executive Order 9066, he heard from some advisers who opposed relocation. A secret report before Pearl Harbor suggested that the U.S. government would not have to fear the Japanese Americans, the Nisei in particular. The report called the Nisei "eager to show...loyalty.... They are not Japanese in culture. They are foreigners to Japan." In early 1942, Roosevelt received other reports that said the United States did not face a security threat on the West Coast from the Japanese Americans living there. The Federal Bureau of Investigation (FBI) said that it had "no substantial evidence of planned sabotage by any alien."

One member of Roosevelt's cabinet who opposed relocation was Attorney General Francis Biddle. He served as the government's top lawyer. Biddle told Roosevelt that the government was probably denying the constitutional rights of the Nisei, since they were U.S. citizens. Still, Biddle did not speak out strongly against the executive order, which he later regretted. In 1944, he wrote that the relocation was "un-American, unconstitutional, and un-Christian."

During the war, thousands of average Americans wrote Roosevelt on a variety of topics. Some opposed the relocation. One letter written in 1943 asked, "Is it reasonable for Japanese Americans to be interned and Germans and Italians, not?" Others asked the president to at least publicly honor the Japanese Americans who had peacefully accepted their internment or volunteered to fight for the country.

Some of the strongest statements against relocation came in the Supreme Court decision in *Korematsu v. United States*. Three justices dissented from the decision that supported relocation. Justice Frank Murphy wrote that it defied reason and logic to assume "that *all* persons of Japanese ancestry may have a dangerous tendency to commit sabotage and espionage." He called the internment "the legalization of racism." Justice Robert Jackson said that General DeWitt may have had a good military reason to relocate the Japanese Americans from the West Coast—but that did not mean it was constitutional.

Fred Korematsu, plaintiff in the Supreme Court case Korematsu v. United States, receives the Presidential Medal of Freedom from President Bill Clinton at the White House in January 1998.

In the decades since World War II, most historians have sided with the critics of relocation. Interning innocent Americans solely because of their ethnic background was one of the U.S. government's worst acts against its own citizens.

THE FIRST LADY'S OPINION

During his four terms as president, Franklin Roosevelt often turned to his wife Eleanor for advice. The first lady believed that enemy aliens were treated unfairly during World War II. Early in 1942, she publicly defended the loyalty of both the Issei and Nisei, and she opposed relocation. The president, however, told her that he did not want to discuss this subject with her.

In Their Own Words

Here is part of Justice Frank Murphy's dissent against the Supreme Court's decision in *Korematsu v. United States*.

No adequate reason is given for the failure to treat these Japanese Americans on an individual basis by holding investigations and hearings to separate the loyal from the disloyal, as was done in the case of persons of German and Italian ancestry.... Nor is there any denial of the fact that not one person of Japanese ancestry was accused or convicted of espionage or sabotage after Pearl Harbor while they were still free.... All residents of this nation are kin in some way by blood or culture to a foreign land. Yet...they must...be treated at all times as the heirs of the American experiment and as entitled to all the rights and freedoms guaranteed by the Constitution.

CHAPTER TWO

Cold War
Anti-Communism

WHAT

Senator Joseph McCarthy and others attempt to remove suspected communists from government service and private organizations.

ISSUES

Protecting the United States from communist spies; protecting the basic freedoms of U.S. citizens

WHERE

Nationwide

WHEN

1947–1954

*D*uring World War II (1939–1945), the Soviet Union and the United States fought as allies against Germany. Their relationship was uneasy, however, since they distrusted each other. The Soviet Union was created in 1917, with the successful communist revolution in Russia. Under communist rule, the Soviet state owned all businesses and most property, and the communist Party controlled the government. The economic and political system that developed in the Soviet Union denied Soviet citizens almost all personal freedom, and Soviet leader Joseph Stalin killed millions of his own people to enforce his complete control.

Most Americans detested communism and its practice in the Soviet Union. The Soviet system opposed U.S. values, which promoted the private ownership of property and free elections of public officials. Americans also knew that the Soviet Union wanted to set up communist states around the world and feared that the Soviets would use any means necessary to destroy the U.S. system of government. After meeting Stalin in 1945, President Harry Truman said that he believed that "the Russians are planning world conquest."

With the end of World War II, the United States and the Soviet Union began what was later called the Cold War. They tried to promote their own political and economic values around the world while hoping to weaken each other's influence. This global struggle was different from an actual "hot" war between two armies. At times, however, Soviet and other communist forces did meet U.S. troops and their allies on the battlefield.

Fast Fact

As practiced in the Soviet Union, communism grew out of the ideas of the nineteenth-century German thinker Karl Marx and the Russian revolutionary leader Vladimir Lenin, the first leader of the Soviet Union. communism is sometimes called Marxist Leninism.

THE FIRST FEARS OF COMMUNISM

Karl Marx developed the theory of communism during the mid-nineteenth century, and even before his ideas were applied in the Soviet Union, some Americans feared communism's presence in the United States. As industry grew in America after the Civil War (1861–1865), more workers wanted to form unions. These organizations struggled for better wages and working conditions for their members. Some people with communist beliefs worked for the unions, so some Americans assumed that all unions had ties to communism and could not be trusted. At the end of World War I (1914–1918), the fear of communism rose again. The Soviet Union had just formed, and the U.S. government began to clamp down on American communists and suspected communists. This period is sometimes called the Red Scare, since communists used the color red in their flags and symbols.

The Hunt for Enemies Within

As early as the 1920s, the Federal Bureau of Investigation (FBI) had tried to track down communist spies. In 1938, the House of Representatives launched a committee eventually called the House Un-American Activities Committee (HUAC) to look for communist influences in the United States. Within ten years, many Americans believed the Soviet Union was a serious danger to U.S. security. In 1947, President Truman issued an order that prevented any known communists or people with a "sympathetic association" to the Communist Party from working for the U.S. government.

In the late 1940s, HUAC turned its attention to Hollywood. Some members of Congress were concerned that the motion picture industry was dominated by communists who were using their influence to spread communist propaganda. HUAC also began investigating the possibility that members of the communist Party had once served or were still serving in the U.S. government. The committee held a series of hearings investigating Alger Hiss, who had worked in the State Department under President Franklin Roosevelt.

Whittaker Chambers, a magazine editor, admitted that, during the 1930s, he had recruited American communists to spy for the Soviet Union. One of the people that he worked with, he claimed, was Hiss, who denied ever being a communist when he appeared before HUAC. Chambers then showed Congress documents that Hiss had given him to give to the Soviets back in 1938. Congress could not charge Hiss with espionage, since too much time had passed since his alleged spying took place, but HUAC did accuse Hiss of perjury, or lying while under oath, and he was convicted in 1950. The Hiss case raised the fear that communists were still operating in the government, threatening the country's security.

Other events during this time added to American fears of communism and potential spies. In 1948, Czech communists working for the Soviet Union took power in Czechoslovakia. The next year, communists won a civil war in China. At almost the same time, the Soviet Union tested its first atomic bomb. This weapon uses the tremendous energy inside the atoms of certain materials to create a huge explosion. (Atoms are the basic units of all matter.) The United States had dropped two atomic bombs on Japan in 1945, ending World War II. Americans worried that the Soviet Union could someday use atomic weapons to destroy the United States and its allies.

The FBI did not charge anyone with spying because it did not catch anyone actually committing espionage. The FBI also lacked a key piece of evidence: information collected from the Venona Project. Venona was the code name for a U.S. government project to intercept messages between Soviet agents in the

United States and their leaders in Moscow, the capital of the Soviet Union. The project began during World War II. However, the U.S. government did not finish translating the messages for decades, and U.S. officials did not release the results of the project until the 1990s. The Venona Project proved that several hundred Americans, including those named by Elizabeth Bentley, an acknowledged Soviet agent, had spied for the Soviet Union.

In 1948, Whittaker Chambers leaves the federal courthouse in New York City, where he faced a grand jury investigating his involvement in subversive activities.

"THE RED SPY QUEEN" AND THE VENONA PROJECT

In 1945, Elizabeth Bentley was the first person engaged in espionage to step forward and name other spies. She had acted as a courier, carrying information between communist spies in Washington, D.C., and New York. Her list of Soviet agents included Alger Hiss and Harry Dexter White. Both men worked for the U.S. government. When the media learned about Bentley and her claims, they nicknamed her "the Red Spy Queen."

Famous Figures

ALGER HISS
(1904–1996)

Alger Hiss (seated) graduated from Harvard Law School in 1929 and worked for several prominent law firms before joining the U.S. government. In 1945, Hiss traveled with President Roosevelt to the Yalta Conference, where the president met with Joseph Stalin and British prime minister Winston Churchill. The leaders discussed their plans for Europe after World War II. Hiss served almost four years in prison for lying to HUAC. He always maintained that he was not a Soviet spy, and many top U.S. officials who believed him attacked his accusers. Years later, the Venona messages seemed to prove his guilt, though some historians say that the proof is not definite. Several former Soviet officials also claim that Hiss never spied for the Soviet Union.

McCarthy Joins the Hunt

The concerns over communism continued in 1950. In February, scientist Klaus Fuchs was arrested for espionage. He was accused of giving the Soviets information on how to build atomic weapons. Fuchs had worked on the Manhattan Project, the secret U.S.-Canadian-British project that had created the first atomic weapons. A few other workers on the project were also arrested. In June, North Korea, a communist government supported by the Soviet Union and China, invaded South Korea, a U.S. ally. President Truman asked the United Nations (UN) to send troops to defend South Korea. The UN was an organization that was formed after World War II to prevent future world wars.

By this time, Senator Joseph McCarthy of Wisconsin was leading his own search for communists in the U.S. government. In a speech on February 9, 1950, McCarthy claimed that he had a list of fifty-seven people who worked in the U.S. State Department and were "either card carrying members or certainly loyal to the Communist Party." In other speeches he gave in 1950, McCarthy said that his list of suspected communists included more than 200 names. The senator said that he wanted "the whole sorry mess of twisted, warped thinkers…swept from the national scene."

At this time, many Republicans—and some Democrats— thought that Truman was not doing enough to fight the Soviet Union around the world or catch communist spies at home. Later in 1950, Truman vetoed a bill designed to limit the role of communist groups or organizations connected to them. Congress passed the bill into law without the president's signature.

McCarthy's efforts led to more investigations of people accused of being communists or of once belonging to the party. McCarthy even attacked General George Marshall, a respected military leader who had also served as secretary of state under Harry Truman. McCarthy said that Marshall had influenced U.S. policies that strengthened communism in Eastern Europe and China.

Famous Figures

JOSEPH McCARTHY
(1908–1957)

Trained as a lawyer, Joseph McCarthy won his first political race in 1939. During World War II, he joined the marines and earned the nickname "Tail-Gunner Joe." McCarthy later lied about his war record to make himself look better to voters back home. In 1946, he was elected to the U.S. Senate, where he was considered energetic. His focus on communists, some historians believe, was part of his continuing effort to win attention from voters and the media. After McCarthy's 1954 hearings that investigated communists in the army, the Senate censured, or publicly criticized, McCarthy for his behavior. By this time, he suffered from alcoholism, which led to his death a few years later.

McCarthyism at Its Peak

By the time that McCarthy emerged as America's leading anti-communist, the Soviet Union had largely stopped its efforts to recruit U.S. government spies. This was because it knew that the U.S. government was reading the Soviet spies' messages to Moscow. Still, Americans, who did not know that the Soviets were limiting their spying efforts, were ready to believe McCarthy. Other Republicans accepted him, too, because they saw that his beliefs were popular with voters. However, none of the people on McCarthy's list of alleged communists in the U.S. government was ever arrested for espionage or proved to be a communist.

McCarthy's name was used to coin a new word: McCarthyism. To the senator's supporters, McCarthyism meant a strong effort to protect America by uncovering communists who threatened to harm it. McCarthy's critics, however, saw McCarthyism as a dangerous development. It rested on making false charges against innocent people, leading to unnecessary fear and suspicion. People who did not support the senator or who held beliefs considered "un-American" risked joining the list of the accused.

McCarthyism went beyond trying to catch communists serving in the U.S. government. The suspicion carried over to university professors, who were sometimes asked to swear their loyalty to the United States to keep their jobs. State and local government officials also looked for possible communist influences among their workers.

McCarthy's role as the leader of the anti-communist movement finally ended in 1954. He accused the U.S. Army of protecting soldiers who might have ties to communism. Army officials refused to help him. In hearings aired on television, McCarthy seemed rude and hostile as he questioned witnesses and the army's lawyer.
A television reporter also released information showing that most of McCarthy's charges against supposed communists were wrong. The senator's popularity fell, and his anti-communist campaign ended. The HUAC hearings and other government investigations, however, continued for several more years.

> *Fast Fact*
>
> During the McCarthy era, textbooks were closely examined. They were criticized or pulled out of schools if they seemed to promote ideas linked to socialism, the economic system in communist states.

The Argument for Hunting communists

McCarthy and other anti-communists believed that communist spies and their supporters threatened the security of the United States. The director of the FBI, J. Edgar Hoover, expressed this belief in 1947 when he told Congress, "There is no doubt as to where a real communist's loyalty rests. Their allegiance is to Russia, not the United States."

The charges made by Elizabeth Bentley, the Hiss case, and the Manhattan Project spies convinced many Americans that communist espionage continued. If the Soviet Union would spy on the United States when they were allies, certainly it would continue spying during the Cold War. The anti-communists believed that loyalty oaths and limits on personal freedom were necessary to protect the American political system. Some Americans argued that the communists were particularly dangerous because they used deceit. They tried to distance themselves from obvious communist groups and seem like loyal Americans. Their tactics, one veterans' group claimed, "make it difficult for the average trusting citizen to keep up with…[their] swindle and con game."

Some of the government actions to fight communism were confirmed by the courts. The Smith Act of 1940 made it illegal to call for the overthrow of the U.S. government. In 1949, some U.S. Communist Party members were found guilty of violating the act, even though they had not actually told anyone to overthrow the government or plotted to do so themselves. Simply by being communists, the government argued, they accepted Marxist Leninist teachings that called for an end to democratic governments. The U.S. Supreme Court agreed that the party's beliefs made it a threat and that the right of free speech and assembly could be limited in this case. "Overthrow of the Government by force and violence," Chief Justice Fred Vinson wrote, "is certainly a substantial enough interest for the Government to limit speech."

Not all anti-communists supported McCarthy and his methods. Some of them did not like the fear that the senator and his followers created. They saw a difference between Americans who voiced genuine criticisms of the government and communists who wanted to overthrow it. Still, these "liberal anti-communists" argued that the country had to actively fight communism. Sidney Hook, a leader of these Americans, wrote in 1952 that communists worked in secrecy to achieve their aims, rather than debating their views in public. He cited the writings of Lenin, who said that communists had to "combine legal with illegal work, legal and illegal organizations.... Illegal work is particularly necessary in the Army, the Navy, and police."

In Their Own Words

Here is part of the speech that Joseph McCarthy gave in February 1950 that first brought him national attention.

The reason why we find ourselves in a position of [weakness] is not because our only powerful, potential enemy has sent men to invade our shores, but rather because of the traitorous actions of those who have been treated so well by this nation.... In my opinion the State Department, which is one of the most important government departments, is thoroughly infested with communists.

McCarthyism's Opponents

The most vocal anti-communists were Republicans, such as Senator McCarthy. They blamed President Harry Truman, a Democrat, for allowing communists to serve in the government. Democrats and liberals defended Truman while attacking the anti-communists. Truman's supporters did not approve of communism or spying. They believed, however, that McCarthy and others were making false accusations and denying the legal rights of Americans.

Truman himself argued for protecting legal rights when he vetoed the 1950 Internal Security Act. Americans had a right to speak their minds freely and hold views that most citizens rejected. Efforts directed against communists denied those rights. Truman especially worried that some groups would be labeled communist merely because they supported some of the same aims that communists did, without actually being connected to the

Communist Party. "It is not enough to say that this would probably not be done," Truman wrote. "The mere fact that it could be done...[creates] opportunities for official condemnation of organizations and individuals for perfectly honest opinions which happen to be stated also by Communists."

Some U.S. courts agreed that loyalty oaths and background checks violated legal guarantees. Under the Constitution, Americans have the right to hold any political beliefs that they want and associate with people who share those beliefs. Thousands of people lost their jobs because they had once belonged to groups suspected of having ties to communists. In some cases, these people never learned what evidence was used against them, and they could not defend themselves against the charges. In several cases, workers or their unions challenged the laws that led to their firing. One case was finally settled in 1955, with the court ruling against the government. The court ruled that "this system of secret informers, whisperers, and tale-bearers" denied the workers their right to receive due process. This right ensures that accused criminals know the evidence being used against them.

In Their Own Words

In 1952, William O. Douglas was a liberal member of the U.S. Supreme Court. He was a strong defender of civil liberties—rights protected under the U.S. Constitution. Here is part of an article that he wrote attacking the extreme anti-communist movement.

When freedom of expression is supreme, a nation will keep its balance and stability.... If we are true to our traditions, if we are tolerant of the whole market place of ideas, we will always be strong. Our weakness grows when we become intolerant of opposing ideas, depart from our standards of civil liberties, and borrow the policeman's philosophy from the enemy we detest.

CHAPTER THREE

Brown

v.

Board of

Education

WHAT
The U.S. Supreme Court ends the policy of
"separate but equal" schooling in the United States.

ISSUES
The legality of separate but equal policies;
the rights of states to have such policies

WHERE
Nationwide

WHEN
1952–1955

*I*n 1896, the U.S. Supreme Court ruled that the state of Louisiana could separate African Americans from whites on public transportation. The decision in the case *Plessy v. Ferguson* said that this kind of segregation was legal, as long as blacks had access to the same kind of transportation as whites. The decision had the effect of legalizing many other attempts by some states—mostly in the South—to keep blacks and whites separate in public areas.

Segregation existed in restaurants, hotels, and hospitals and at public drinking fountains and pools. The most damaging segregation, however, may have come in education. Black and white students attended separate schools, and the quality of the education was not equal, as it was supposed to be under the law. Towns spent much less on education for African American children, and many of their teachers lacked proper training. These students also sometimes had to travel much farther than white students to reach their schools, because many towns built fewer schools for blacks.

Starting in the 1930s, an organization called the National Association for the Advancement of Colored People (NAACP) began to challenge separate but equal policies in education. Its lawyers worked out a specific plan: They would attack segregation starting at the top of the education system, in universities. They believed that the U.S. Supreme Court would be more likely to rule in their favor in these cases, because Southern states had a poor record in establishing separate but equal graduate schools—schools that college students can attend after earning a four-year degree. Then the lawyers would work their way down to where the problem was the worst, in elementary schools. The NAACP later set up a separate agency, the Legal Defense Fund (LDF), to work on the legal issues related to ending segregation.

Fast Fact

The system of separate but equal laws in the South was often called "Jim Crow." This name came from a nineteenth-century African American stage character who was played by a white actor in black makeup.

The first lead attorney for the NAACP was Charles Houston, a law professor from Howard University in Washington, D.C. In addition to doing legal research, he wrote articles arguing that African Americans should fight for more money for their children's education and the end of segregation. He hoped that one day blacks would not have to fight in courts for their rights. During one trial he said, "We'll all be better off when instead of spending money in lawsuits we spend it for social advancement." Houston's most famous student was Thurgood Marshall. He worked with Houston at the NAACP and later ran the LDF. Marshall would argue some of the most famous cases that challenged segregation.

Fast Fact

In 1940, several Southern states spent only one dollar on public education for black students for every three dollars that the states spent for white students.

Famous Figures

THURGOOD MARSHALL
(1908–1993)

The great-grandson of a slave, Thurgood Marshall directly experienced segregation in his hometown of Baltimore, Maryland. After earning a law degree, he began a lifelong effort to secure civil rights for African Americans. These rights included voting and receiving equal treatment in the workforce, courts, and schools. Marshall's work with the NAACP and LDF led to several important court victories, topped off with the decision in *Brown v. Board of Education*. In 1967, Marshall became the first African American named to the U.S. Supreme Court.

Slow Progress

In 1938, Houston and Marshall represented Lloyd Gaines before the U.S. Supreme Court. Gaines wanted to enter the University of Missouri Law School, which was segregated. The

state did not have a law school for African Americans. State officials said that they would build one and that in the meantime they would help pay for Gaines's schooling in another state. The NAACP lawyers did not argue that separate but equal schooling was unconstitutional. Instead, they argued that education opportunities for blacks had to be truly equal. The Supreme Court agreed that promising to build a school or to send Gaines out of state did not give him an equal chance to study law in Missouri. The court ruled against the state.

A little more than ten years later, Marshall and the LDF won two more important cases. Both dealt with black men seeking to enter graduate schools. In *Sweatt v. Painter*, the Supreme Court ruled that Texas had to let a black student attend the University of Texas Law School. In *McLaurin v. Oklahoma State Regents*, the court ruled in favor of George McLaurin. Oklahoma officials had let him attend graduate school, but he had to sit apart from the white students in classrooms, the library, and the cafeteria. The court wrote that this segregation limited McLaurin's "ability to study, to engage in discussion and exchange views with other students, and, in general, to learn his profession."

Lawyers George E.C. Hayes (left), Thurgood Marshall (center), and James Nabrit on the steps of the U.S. Supreme Court in May 1954. They led the fight before the Supreme Court to abolish segregation in public schools.

Briggs and Brown

In 1950, a group of black parents in Clarendon County, South Carolina, claimed that their children—a majority in the school district—received much worse schooling than the county's white children. They went to court in a case called *Briggs v. Elliot*.

Harry Briggs was one of the parents, and Roderick Elliot led the local board of education.

Marshall argued the case in front of a group of three federal judges. He noted that the black schools in Clarendon County were small wooden shacks with no indoor toilets. The white schools were larger, better built, and had many more educational supplies. The county also spent more than three times as much on the white students as on the blacks. Still, two of the three judges ruled that separate but equal policies were legal, though they did order Clarendon County to improve the schools for the black students. The one judge who dissented was J. Waties Waring, who wrote, "Segregation in education can never produce equality…and is an evil that must be [ended]."

A few days later, on June 25, 1951, another segregation case began. Black and white students in Topeka, Kansas, attended separate schools. Although the schools were not as unequal as the schools in Clarendon County, some African American parents disliked the arrangement. Linda Brown was one of many African American children who had to travel across the city to attend a black elementary school instead of being able to attend a white school much closer to her home. Her father and several other black parents worked with the NAACP to challenge segregation in Topeka.

In this case, a federal court admitted that "segregation…in public schools has a [negative] effect upon colored children." Still, the judges all agreed that the law in Kansas did not violate the separate but equal doctrine as laid down in *Plessy v. Ferguson.* Marshall and the NAACP then decided to ask the U.S. Supreme Court to review this ruling and the one from *Briggs v. Elliot.* In June 1952, the Court agreed, and later it combined three more public school segregation cases with these two. Collectively, all the cases were known as *Brown v. Board of Education of Topeka, Kansas.*

Fast Fact

In 1948, President Harry Truman took a large step toward ending segregation in the United States when he ordered the military to integrate white and black troops. The first integrated units saw action during the Korean War (1950–1953).

THE REACH OF SEGREGATION

During the 1940s and early 1950s, laws regarding segregation in public schools varied. Seventeen states required towns and cities to have separate but equal schools. Four states, including Kansas, let local officials decide whether or not to segregate students by race. Public schools were also segregated in Washington, D.C. In many other states, separate but equal schooling was de facto—it was not spelled out in the laws but still existed because of various social and economic reasons. These included racism and the difficulty that African Americans had earning enough money to move into neighborhoods or towns with good schools.

The Supreme Court Decides

In May 1954, Chief Justice Earl Warren announced the Supreme Court's decision. On a vote of nine to nothing, the Court ruled that segregation in public schools was illegal. The key issue, according to Warren, was whether separate schooling for blacks denied them a truly equal education. Warren wrote, "We believe that it does." This decision meant that states would have to integrate their schools and that other forms of public segregation were also illegal. The ruling in *Plessy v. Ferguson* that had allowed separate but equal policies was now overturned.

Fast Fact

Legal scholars sometimes refer to the 1954 decision ending segregation as *Brown I.* The second decision on how to achieve it is called *Brown II.*

However, the Supreme Court's ruling in *Brown* did not end the case. The Court ordered a second set of hearings to help it decide how segregation would end. A system that had been in place for decades could not be taken apart overnight. The NAACP wanted schools integrated as quickly as possible. In 1955, the Court ruled that the states should use "all deliberate speed" to end segregation.

The Supreme Court had used the phrase "all deliberate speed" in an earlier decision. Although supporters of integration thought the words were not specific enough,

Warren felt that "all deliberate speed" was the best that the Court could order at the time, since "there were so many blocks preventing an immediate solution of the thing in reality." Some states, however, were able to delay ending segregation for decades.

Famous Figures

EARL WARREN
(1891–1974)

Earl Warren is one of the most controversial chief justices in the history of the Supreme Court. Although trained as a lawyer, Warren did not have any experience as a judge when President Dwight Eisenhower named him chief justice in 1953. He had been governor of California before taking his new position. Warren's supporters praised him for pushing the Court to take a more active role in promoting individual rights and freedoms. His critics believed that Warren went too far in using the Court to shape laws, a responsibility that should have been left to the states and to Congress. Warren is best remembered for coming out strongly against segregation in *Brown v. Board of Education of Topeka, Kansas*. He then convinced all the other justices on the Court to vote his way.

The Argument against Segregation

With the *Brown* case, Marshall and the NAACP decided that they had to stop pushing for merely improving education for segregated black students. Instead, they wanted to strike at the heart of the *Plessy* decision, which made separate but equal a national legal policy. Marshall wanted to show that segregated schools could never be equal for African Americans. Their education would always be worse than what white students received in their own schools.

To argue this point, Marshall repeated some of the evidence showing that the physical conditions in many schools for blacks were much worse than those in schools for whites. He also tried to prove that this inequality had a bad effect on black children. To argue this, the NAACP legal team relied on research carried out by a variety of social scientists. Some of this evidence had been used when *Briggs v. Elliot* was first argued in 1951.

For that trial, Dr. Kenneth Clark had studied black children who had gone to segregated schools. He found that the students had a poor self-image—they tended to think that being white was better than being black. As Clark later put it, "These children saw themselves as inferior." The NAACP lawyers argued that those feelings were the result of segregation and that children who felt inferior would not learn as well as ones who felt good about themselves. Marshall said, "The Negro child is made to go to an inferior school, he is branded in his own mind as inferior…which prevents his ever feeling he is equal."

Marshall also focused on the Fourteenth Amendment to the Constitution. Congress and the states had added this amendment after the Civil War (1861–1865). Its main goal was to give African Americans the same rights as whites. State governments could not deny blacks "equal protection of the laws." The amendment was aimed at so-called Black Codes, laws passed in Southern states that limited the legal rights of black citizens. Marshall argued that segregation laws were similar to the old Black Codes because they both violated the idea of equal protection.

Once the Supreme Court ruled in favor of Brown and the NAACP, African Americans hailed the decision. So did whites who believed that separate but equal policies violated the Constitution. Some Americans also thought that the *Brown* decision had an important impact beyond the United States. At the time, the United States and the Soviet Union were fighting the Cold War. The two sides tried to influence events around the world so that other countries would support their policies. Americans argued that their political system stood for equality and freedom. Segregation, however, seemed to show that

Americans did not always follow their own ideals. An African American newspaper argued that ending segregation was good for U.S. foreign policy: "[The *Brown* decision] will effectively impress upon millions of colored people in Asia and Africa the fact that idealism and social morality can and do prevail in the United States, regardless of race, creed, or color."

THE SWEDISH CONNECTION

One of the social scientists who played an indirect role in *Brown v. Board of Education* was Swedish economist Gunnar Myrdal. In 1944, he published a two-volume work called *An American Dilemma,* a detailed study of segregation and race relations in the United States. He argued that local officials in Southern states were denying African Americans their constitutional rights. The NAACP cited *An American Dilemma* as it tried to prove that segregation always had a lasting negative effect on black children. Earl Warren also referred to Myrdal's work in his decision on *Brown I.*

In Their Own Words

Here is part of the argument that Thurgood Marshall made to the U.S. Supreme Court in 1953.

The only way that this Court can decide this case [against us], is that there must be some reason which gives the state the right to make a classification [based on race]...and we submit the only way to arrive at this decision is to find for some reason that Negroes are inferior to all other human beings.... The only [reason for segregation] is [a]...determination that the people who were formerly in slavery, regardless of anything else, shall be kept as near that stage as possible, and now is the time, we submit, that this Court should make it clear that that is not what our Constitution stands for.

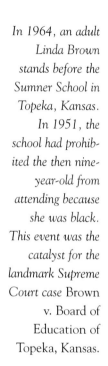

In 1964, an adult Linda Brown stands before the Sumner School in Topeka, Kansas. In 1951, the school had prohibited the then nine-year-old from attending because she was black. This event was the catalyst for the landmark Supreme Court case Brown v. Board of Education of Topeka, Kansas.

Support for Separate but Equal

The five cases combined under *Brown v. Board of Education of Topeka, Kansas* came from several states and Washington, D.C. Most of the states were in the South, where segregation in schools was required by law. The states believed that they had a legal right to order segregation, as outlined in *Plessy v. Ferguson,* and that the decision in that 1896 case was constitutional.

The lead attorney for the *Brown* defense was John W. Davis, who represented Clarendon County, South Carolina, home of Harry Briggs. When he spoke at the Supreme Court hearings in 1952, Davis argued that a state had the right to classify and separate students in many ways—age, sex, mental abilities, or race. That separation was legal, as long as the education was equal. He also pointed out that over the years, the Supreme Court had considered several cases that addressed the separate but equal policy. Each time, the Court had upheld it. Davis then dismissed the claims of the NAACP experts who said that segregated schools were always unequal because of the damage they did to black children. Davis said that the evidence "was in conflict with the opinion of other and better informed sources."

The Fourteenth Amendment was at the heart of Thurgood Marshall's case. Davis tried to weaken Marshall's position by citing past court decisions. Davis quoted one decision that said the justices had to consider the "common understanding" of an issue at the time that a constitutional amendment was proposed. When Congress passed the Fourteenth Amendment, it allowed segregated schooling in Washington, D.C. Many states that approved the amendment also had segregated schools. To Davis, this meant that the lawmakers did not intend for "equal protection" to prevent segregated schools.

Davis also tried to argue that some African Americans supported segregation. He quoted an article written by W.E.B. Du Bois, a leading African American scholar. Du Bois had written in 1935 that separate schools for blacks and whites were "infinitely better" than sending black children to white schools, where they would be mistreated. Davis, however, did not mention that Du Bois actually preferred integrated schools where black children would be treated equally.

Finally, Davis closed by saying that state and local control of schools was an important part of the American political system. The states had the legal right to decide how schools should be run. Parents, both black and white, had a right to decide the issue so that their children were not "forced into what may be an unwelcome contract."

When the Supreme Court reached its decision in *Brown*, people who supported segregation reacted angrily. Georgia governor Herman Talmadge said that the Court was denying the states the right to manage their own affairs. Other Southern politicians and newspapers shared this view. Some people who favored segregation began to criticize the NAACP, accusing it of being tied to communists in the United States. The NAACP's foes wanted Americans to think that integration was part of a communist plot to weaken the nation's traditional political values.

Some political leaders who privately opposed the Court's ruling did not speak out against it. These politicians included President Dwight Eisenhower. In public, he said that he would enforce the decision, as he was required to do under the Constitution, but in private, he said that the public was not ready for integrated schools. In both the North and South, many whites failed to support integration, thereby stalling the process of truly ending the separate but equal doctrine.

In Their Own Words

In 1956, more than 100 members of Congress issued a statement attacking the Supreme Court's rulings in the two *Brown* decisions. Here is part of that statement.

The original Constitution does not mention education. Neither does the Fourteenth Amendment nor any other amendment. The debates preceding the submission of the Fourteenth Amendment clearly show that there was no intent that it should affect the system of education maintained by the states.... This unwarranted exercise of power by the Court, contrary to the Constitution, is creating chaos and confusion in the states principally affected. It is destroying the [friendly] relations between the white and Negro races that have been created through ninety years of patient effort by the good people of both races. It has planted hatred and suspicion where there had been...friendship and understanding.

CHAPTER FOUR

The Vietnam War

WHAT

*The United States sends hundreds of thousands of troops to help
South Vietnam battle North Vietnam.*

ISSUES

*Stopping the spread of communism in Asia; the need for U.S.
involvement; the legality of certain military actions*

WHERE

Nationwide

WHEN

1965–1975

After World War II (1939–1945), U.S. foreign policy centered on stopping the spread of communism around the world. The leading communist nation was the Soviet Union. Its leaders had openly talked about destroying capitalism, the economic system that was practiced in the United States and many other nations. The Soviet leaders wanted to introduce communism wherever they could. That effort and the U.S. struggle to stop it were called the Cold War.

In 1949, China joined the Soviet Union as a communist nation. U.S. leaders feared that the two countries would work together to spread communism in Asia. In 1950, troops from North Korea, a communist nation supported by the Soviet Union and China, attacked South Korea, a U.S. ally. President Harry Truman convinced the United Nations (UN) to send troops to Asia to help the South Koreans battle their northern enemy. For three years, soldiers from the United States and more than a dozen other nations fought communist troops in Korea.

At the same time, Vietnam was trying to win its independence from France. The French had ruled Vietnam since the 1860s, except during World War II, when Japan seized control. Vietnamese forces, led by Ho Chi Minh, had fought the Japanese during the war, and Ho had declared Vietnamese independence in 1945. The French, however, wanted to keep Vietnam as a colony.

Ho was a nationalist—he wanted to end any foreign control over his people. He was also a dedicated communist who had studied in the Soviet Union. U.S. leaders distrusted Ho and assumed that he would take orders from China and the Soviet Union. Under Truman, the United States followed a policy called containment—containing communism where it already existed and trying to stop its spread to other countries, such as Vietnam. In 1950, Truman gave France money to help it fight Ho and keep control of Vietnam.

> *Fast Fact*
> Ho Chi Minh's declaration of independence for Vietnam in 1946 was modeled on the U.S. Declaration of Independence of 1776.

> ## FRENCH INDOCHINA
>
> In 1950, Vietnam was part of a region called French Indochina, which also included Cambodia and Laos. These three countries are part of the larger Asian region called Indochina, which also includes Thailand, Myanmar, and part of Malaysia. This region is also sometimes called Southeast Asia.

Growing Involvement in Indochina

When the Korean War ended in 1953, France was still battling Ho's forces. President Dwight Eisenhower continued to aid the French. Despite this help, France could not defeat Ho, and Vietnam won its independence in 1954. Soon, the country was split in two, with Ho ruling the north and Ngo Dinh Diem controlling the south. The U.S. government supported Diem, who was strongly anti-communist. He was also corrupt, and he often mistreated his people in his effort to keep communism out of South Vietnam. He tortured or killed political enemies and arrested innocent people. (In the north, Ho had earlier carried out similar harsh policies against his enemies.) Diem's actions turned many South Vietnamese against him and his government. The communists, who wanted to unite the two Vietnams under their rule, took advantage of this anger. They recruited soldiers and supporters to fight the government in the south. The South Vietnamese who embraced this effort were eventually called the Viet Cong.

Under Eisenhower, the United States sent money and supplies to help Diem gain control in the south and fight the Viet Cong. The Americans also sent about 900 military advisers. When John Kennedy took over as president in 1961, he continued Eisenhower's policies and gradually sent more advisers. These U.S. soldiers were supposed to train the South Vietnamese. They also flew helicopters that carried the South Vietnamese into battle. The Americans themselves were not supposed to fight, but at times, some of them did fire on the Viet Cong.

By the time that Kennedy took office, U.S. officials were also concerned about Laos. The North Vietnamese were aiding communists there, and they sent supplies through Laos and neighboring Cambodia to help the Viet Cong. The problems in Southeast Asia seemed to be growing. Kennedy was determined to end the communist threat, but he wanted to do it without sending regular U.S. military forces. He hoped more money and more advisers would help Diem defeat the communists.

THE VOTE THAT NEVER WAS

The agreement that ended Vietnam's war with France was called the Geneva Accords. Under the accords, North and South Vietnam were supposed to hold elections in July 1956 to choose a leader for a reunited nation. Diem, however, refused to hold these elections. He and U.S. leaders knew that Ho would likely win a national election, guaranteeing a communist government in Vietnam. Diem and the Americans wanted to keep a separate, anti-communist government in the south.

Johnson's War

In November 1963, Kennedy was assassinated, and Vice President Lyndon B. Johnson took over the presidency. Like Kennedy, "LBJ," as he was called, did not want direct U.S. military involvement in Southeast Asia. At the same time, Johnson believed that the United States had to continue its struggle to end communism there.

In August 1964, Congress gave Johnson broad powers to fight communism in Vietnam, though the lawmakers did not officially declare war. Instead, they instructed Johnson "to take all necessary steps, including the use of armed force," to protect the freedom of South Vietnam and other countries of the region that asked for help. Within six months, Johnson ordered the first large-scale bombing of targets in North Vietnam. Then on March 8, 1965, the first regular U.S. ground troops arrived in South Vietnam, joining the thousands of U.S. advisers already serving there.

By the end of 1965, almost 200,000 U.S. troops were in South Vietnam, and North Vietnamese troops were helping the Viet Cong fight both the South Vietnamese and the Americans. The U.S. forces had better weapons, but the Viet Cong had several advantages. They could blend in with civilians and avoid the U.S. troops. The Americans often had trouble telling who was their enemy. Because the Americans sometimes killed civilians, they lost support among the South Vietnamese people. The South Vietnamese government was also a problem for the United States. Diem, who had often refused to follow U.S. orders, was assassinated in 1963. The rulers who followed him were just as corrupt, and they continued to lose the loyalty of many South Vietnamese.

As the Vietnam War (1964–1975) went on, Americans began to speak out against it. Thousands of college students protested the war at large rallies. Some scholars and journalists said that the U.S. government was lying about how well the war was going and that the Americans could never win. Military leaders, meanwhile, said that they could win the war—if they had enough troops and unlimited political support. Johnson, however, sometimes pulled back from giving the military everything that it wanted. He feared the rising cost of the war and the growing public opinion against it.

The low point for Johnson came in January 1968, when the North Vietnamese launched a series of surprise attacks in major

By 1965, protest against America's involvement in the Vietnam War was already building. In Texas, antiwar protesters rally on the road leading to President Johnson's ranch.

cities across South Vietnam. The North Vietnamese hoped that more civilians would join the war against the Americans and South Vietnamese government. The people, however, did not respond as the communists had hoped. The communists also lost thousands of their best troops as the Americans fought back. Thus, the so-called Tet Offensive failed. Still, many Americans saw Tet as a defeat for the United States. The attacks seemed to show that the communists had great power in the south. U.S. public support for the war fell, and that spring, Johnson announced that he would not run again for president.

The North Vietnamese army was well-armed and well-organized. This photograph shows U.S. Marines in 1968, battling communists in Hue, on the Perfume River. American troops fought for five straight days to no avail. The North Vietnamese held on to a significant portion of the city.

THE GULF OF TONKIN

Congress's decision to let President Johnson conduct military actions in Vietnam came after an incident in the Gulf of Tonkin. U.S. warships patrolled this body of water off the east coast of North Vietnam. In late July 1964, South Vietnamese sailors carried out attacks on several North Vietnamese islands. The USS *Maddox* was sent to gather information on how the North Vietnamese responded to these attacks. On August 2, 1964, the North Vietnamese fired on the *Maddox*. Two days later, sailors on the *Maddox* and another U.S. ship, the *Turner Joy*, thought that they were again under attack. In response, U.S. forces soon struck several North Vietnamese targets. Years later, Americans learned that the second attack on the U.S. ships had never taken place; the sailors had made a mistake when they thought that the North Vietnamese had fired torpedoes at their ships. At the time, Johnson did not know all the details of the second incident in the Gulf of Tonkin. Still, he claimed that the incident showed that he needed more power to strike back at the North Vietnamese.

Nixon Takes Control

Richard Nixon, who won the presidential election in November 1968, promised to end the war. His major plan was called Vietnamization: The United States would increase its aid to the South Vietnamese military so it could take over more of the fighting. At the same time, the United States would begin to pull out its own troops. For this plan to work, Nixon thought, the United States first had to expand the war by attacking Viet Cong bases and supply routes in Cambodia and Laos. Nixon began bombing raids on those two countries. He kept the raids secret so that he would not anger Americans who opposed the war.

In 1970, Nixon sent U.S. troops into Cambodia. This time, he told the U.S. public about the military attack. In Cambodia, he said, North Vietnam was "building up to launch massive attacks on our forces and those of South Viet-Nam." U.S. forces had to defeat those troops to make sure that Vietnamization could continue.

As the war went on, the U.S. government held peace talks with the North Vietnamese. The most important talks were held in secret, between Henry Kissinger, Nixon's national security adviser, and Le Duc Tho, a top North Vietnamese official. Meeting in Paris, France, they finally worked out an agreement in January 1973. By this time, Vietnamization was almost complete, and most U.S. troops had left Vietnam. The Paris agreement did not completely protect South Vietnam from further communist attacks, but as Kissinger said to one assistant, "What do you want us to do? Stay there forever?"

The last U.S. combat troops left South Vietnam that year, but the Vietnam War lasted until April 1975. The communists, breaking their agreement to work with the South Vietnamese, kept fighting until they defeated their enemy. As part of the peace agreement, the United States had promised to give South Vietnam huge amounts of military aid. Congress, however, did not go along with the plan, since many Americans believed that the United States had already spent too much money and lost too many lives fighting in Vietnam. Without U.S. aid, South Vietnam had no chance to defeat the communists.

COLD WAR DIPLOMACY

The Vietnam War led to historic diplomatic missions for President Nixon. The Soviet Union and China provided crucial aid to North Vietnam. Nixon and Kissinger hoped that better U.S. relations with the Chinese and Soviets would convince them to put pressure on North Vietnam to end the war. In February 1972, Nixon became the first U.S. president to visit China since it had come under Communist rule. He followed that with a trip to the Soviet Union. Nixon had been a strong anti-communist throughout his political career, but he saw the value of trying to improve relations with his Cold War foes.

The Arguments for War

To some Americans, the situation in Vietnam was similar to the conditions that had led to World War II. During the late 1930s, Germany was controlled by its ruling party, the Nazis, and used its military might to extend its control in Central Europe. Similarly, China and the Soviet Union, each controlled by the communists, tried to extend their military power in Indochina. Also, like Nazi Germany, the Soviet Union and China created what are called totalitarian governments: They severely limited personal freedoms and arrested, tortured, and killed their political enemies. Some American

Fast Fact

The United States spent $150 billion fighting in Southeast Asia, and more than 58,000 Americans were killed during the Vietnam War.

supporters of the Vietnam War believed that totalitarian governments always had to be stopped with force because they did not respect law or diplomacy. These people believed that the United States had to confront the communists in Southeast Asia to defend the ideas of democratic government and its laws.

In 1954, Eisenhower explained the threat to the United States if Southeast Asia became communist. The region had valuable natural resources, such as tin and rubber, and a communist takeover could limit American interests there. Eisenhower also said that communist rule would end the political freedom of the citizens. Most importantly, the loss of Vietnam to the communists could have a "domino effect." The communists there, with Soviet and Chinese aid, would influence neighboring countries and perhaps create revolutions that would spread communism even farther. Then such important U.S. allies as Japan and the Philippines would also face a communist threat. Eisenhower said, "The possible consequences of the loss are just incalculable to the free world."

> *Fast Fact*
>
> According to public opinion polls, popular support for the Vietnam War peaked during 1967, when many Americans favored increasing the military effort.

As time went on, U.S. leaders saw another reason to increase the U.S. presence in Southeast Asia. In 1965, Johnson explained to the American public why he had sent the first combat troops to South Vietnam and why he was ready to send more. "We have made," he said, "a national pledge to help South Viet-Nam defend its independence. And I intend to keep that promise." If the United States did not fight the communists and keep its promise, other U.S. allies might not trust future U.S. promises to them. In addition, the Soviet Union and China might think that the United States was weak. U.S. leaders wanted their Cold War foes to know that the United States was serious about fighting communism. Otherwise, the Chinese and Soviets might take greater risks to try to spread communism.

In Their Own Words

___

In a speech given in November 1969, Richard Nixon explained his policy of Vietnamization and why the United States could not pull out all its troops from Southeast Asia. Here is part of that speech.

Three American Presidents have recognized the great stakes involved in Viet-Nam and understood what had to be done…. For the future of peace…withdrawal would thus be a disaster of immense [size].

- *A nation cannot remain great if it betrays its allies and lets down its friends.*

- *Our defeat and humiliation in South Viet-Nam without question would promote recklessness…[by] those great powers who have not yet abandoned their goals of world conquest.*

- *This would spark violence wherever our commitments help maintain the peace—in the Middle East, in Berlin, eventually even in the Western Hemisphere.*

Ultimately, this would cost more lives. It would not bring peace; it would bring more war.

Opposing the War in Southeast Asia

Historians have talked about the antiwar movement that developed during the Vietnam War. This movement grew dramatically as more U.S. troops went to Southeast Asia and the United States seemed no closer to winning the war. The movement, however, was diverse, with different individuals and groups having different reasons for opposing the war. Some were pacifists—people who oppose all wars and violence of any kind. A larger number had specific reasons for opposing the Vietnam War in particular.

When the first U.S. troops landed in South Vietnam in March 1965, most Americans knew little about Vietnam or the U.S. role there. Soon, however, a group of college students came out against the war. Students for a Democratic Society (SDS) opposed many U.S. government policies of the era. The group believed that President Johnson should focus on ending poverty and inequality at home instead of fighting in Southeast Asia. Some members supported socialism, the economic system practiced in North Vietnam and other communist nations.

During the Vietnam War, U.S. military service was not voluntary, as it is now. In October 1965, SDS released a statement opposing the draft—the government's selection of young men to serve in the military. SDS encouraged young men to become conscientious objectors, or declare that they could not fight in Vietnam for moral reasons. SDS said that Americans should "build a democracy at home and overseas" and not "burn and torture in Vietnam." SDS and other student groups organized large rallies to oppose the draft and the war. Some draft resisters argued that the war was illegal, since Congress had not voted to declare war, as it was supposed to do under the U.S. Constitution.

As the war went on, some returning soldiers joined the antiwar movement. They had direct knowledge of what the U.S. military was doing to innocent civilians. Thousands of South Vietnamese, including women and children, were killed or injured by U.S. troops. Civilians face dangers in any war, but at times, U.S. soldiers deliberately killed the South Vietnamese. One soldier told a group of senators that the military sometimes lied about how many people were killed and wrongly blamed the Viet Cong for damage caused by the United States. The soldier expressed the opinion of many Americans who opposed the war: "There is nothing in South Vietnam which could happen that realistically threatens the United States of America."

The war's opponents included well-known Americans and some political leaders. In 1965, George Ball, one of Johnson's advisers, tried to convince him not to send combat troops to South Vietnam. "Once large numbers of U.S. troops are committed to direct combat, they will begin to take heavy casualties in a war they are ill-equipped to fight in a non-cooperative if not downright hostile countryside." Ball and others believed that the United States could not win the war without large losses, especially since the North Vietnamese were so determined and had strong South Vietnamese support. To many Vietnamese, the war was about driving out another foreign invader and choosing their own form of government, not about the Cold War.

As opposition to the Vietnam War increased, some organizations questioned the constitutional right of Congress to enforce the draft. In 1969, protester Ken Love burned his draft card, demonstrating his intention to avoid fighting the war for America.

Some African American leaders also spoke out against the Vietnam War. Young black men were serving—and dying—in large numbers. Young men could avoid the draft by going to college, but fewer blacks could afford to go, compared to whites. Martin Luther King Jr. was one famous black leader who opposed the war. He believed that blacks were dying overseas while the U.S. government refused to grant them equal rights at home. The black soldiers, King said, were sent "8,000 miles [12,800 kilometers] away to guarantee liberties in Southeast Asia which they had not found in Southwest Georgia." King and others also thought that the U.S. government was spending too much money on the war. That money could have been used to improve the lives of poor Americans.

In Their Own Words

Robert F. Kennedy served as the U.S. attorney general under his brother, John F. Kennedy, and under Lyndon Johnson. In 1968, Robert Kennedy was a U.S. senator who hoped to be the Democratic Party's presidential candidate. By this time, he opposed the Vietnam War. Here is part of an article that Kennedy wrote shortly after the Tet Offensive.

Every detached observer has testified to the enormous corruption [in]…South Vietnamese official life. Hundreds of millions of dollars are stolen by private individuals and government officials while the American people are being asked to pay higher taxes to finance our assistance effort…. Perhaps we could live with corruption [by itself]…. However, the consequence is not simply the loss of American lives. For government corruption is the source of the enemy's strength. It is, more than anything else, the reason why the greatest power on earth cannot defeat a tiny and primitive foe.

THE PENTAGON PAPERS

One person who became famous for his antiwar activity was Daniel Ellsberg. Ellsberg originally worked at the Pentagon, the headquarters of the U.S. Department of Defense. Later, while working for a private company, he helped prepare a secret report on the Vietnam War. The report showed that President Johnson and his advisers had lied about their plans to send combat troops to Southeast Asia. Ellsberg gave a copy of the document to a reporter, and in 1971, several newspapers eventually published these "Pentagon Papers." President Nixon asked the U.S. Supreme Court to stop the release of the Pentagon Papers, but the Court refused. Nixon feared that Americans might question his Vietnam policies if they knew that they had been lied to in the past.

CHAPTER FIVE

Roe v. Wade

WHAT
*The U.S. Supreme Court rules
that abortion is legal, with some limits.*

ISSUES
*A woman's right to choose what to do
about her pregnancy; the morality of abortion*

WHERE
Nationwide

WHEN
1973

For thousands of years, women have sometimes chosen to end their pregnancies before giving birth. This practice is called an abortion. In ancient times, many women drank herbal mixtures that would kill the fetuses—the unborn, developing babies inside them. This practice continued in colonial America. By the nineteenth century, abortion providers in the United States advertised their services in newspapers. Most abortions took place before "quickening" occurred—before the mother could feel the baby moving inside her. Quickening usually happens some time between the fourth and sixth months of a pregnancy.

Women might choose to have an abortion, or husbands or other family members might force them to end a pregnancy. In either case, several factors might influence this decision. A woman's health might be in danger if she delivers a fully developed baby. Poor women who already have children may decide that they cannot afford to raise another child. Other women do not want to go through the effort of childbirth and raising a baby. Unmarried women often choose abortions to avoid a perceived breach of common social practices. Until recent decades, most Americans thought it was wrong for unmarried people to have sexual relations and for unmarried women to have babies. Laws in some states made it illegal for unmarried people to have sex, or for married people to have sex with anyone other than their spouses.

Making Abortion a Crime

By tradition, a fetus was considered a true person only after quickening occurred. Before then, most people thought, the fetus was not truly human and abortion was acceptable. In general, abortions done before quickening were legal until the nineteenth century. An abortion after quickening could be a crime if the fetus were viable, or able to live on its own outside of the mother. Even in these cases, however, courts could not know for sure that a fetus died because of an induced abortion instead of a spontaneous one. Abortion providers could also be arrested if the mother was injured or killed during the procedure.

In 1803, Great Britain passed the first modern law making all abortions illegal. Starting in the 1820s, several U.S. states made it a crime for abortion providers to induce abortions after quickening; other states outlawed all abortions. In most cases, the states were trying to protect the mothers from unskilled abortionists who might hurt them. The mother was not arrested for seeking an abortion. Women could also legally continue to have abortions on their own, without outside help.

Starting in the 1840s, professionally trained doctors began to lead the fight for stricter antiabortion laws. Until that time, most abortions were performed by healers who studied traditional medical methods. Some of these healers were midwives—women who assisted mothers during childbirth and also provided other health care for women. Such healers did not go to schools to

Fast Fact

An abortion caused by surgery or drugs is called an induced abortion. A spontaneous abortion occurs when a fetus dies inside the mother on its own. This is also called a miscarriage.

study science, as doctors did. The doctors argued that the healers often hurt or killed pregnant women during abortions. Some doctors also claimed that the fetus was a patient just as much as the mother was. Past attitudes had focused mostly on the mother's health and desires.

The doctors who called for stricter laws insisted that only doctors, not midwives, should perform abortions and decide when abortions were necessary. Many of these medical professionals reflected the common attitudes about sex and pregnancy during the era. Women who had sex outside of marriage were immoral. Even married women who chose abortions could be considered immoral. As the American Medical Association (AMA) wrote in 1871, such a woman "yields to the pleasure" of sexual relations with her husband, "but shrinks from the pains and responsibilities of [motherhood]." The Roman Catholic Church and many Protestant ministers joined the doctors in their effort to severely limit legal abortions.

By 1900, all states had responded to this effort by making abortion illegal at any time during a pregnancy, though most state laws did allow therapeutic exceptions. For the first time, many states also said that women could be arrested if they tried to perform abortions on themselves. Courts also made it easier to convict people accused of providing abortions. In some cases, lawyers did not need to have eyewitnesses or confessions to convict an accused woman or abortion provider.

Fast Fact

In 1872, Congress acted on the abortion issue, making it illegal to print or bring into the country any information on how to prevent a birth (birth control) or how to abort a fetus.

A MOTHER'S HEALTH

New York's abortion law, passed in 1828, made abortion with outside help illegal, except if a woman's life would be threatened by delivering her baby. This came to be called "the therapeutic exception," and many future abortion laws included similar wording.

Conditions before *Roe v. Wade*

The laws against abortion did not end the practice. Instead, doctors and other people—some skilled, some not—offered secret, illegal abortions. By the middle of the twentieth century, an estimated 500,000 to 1 million illegal abortions took place each year. (By contrast, the number of legal abortions was between 8,000 and 10,000.) The illegal abortions often occurred in dirty offices or private homes, increasing the mother's risk of becoming ill. Each year, as many as 5,000 women died during these "backroom" abortions, or from trying to abort themselves with coat hangers or other objects. Doctors who performed secret abortions risked being arrested and losing their right to practice medicine.

Despite the legal restrictions, many women came to doctors seeking abortions. Some doctors referred such women to safe abortion providers. Many doctors also began to call for easing the restrictions on abortions. Medical opinions had changed by this time, because doctors saw that women would have abortions whether they were legal or not, and the doctors wanted the abortions to be safe. A group of doctors who favored a woman's right to choose an abortion created the Association for the Study of Abortion in 1965. By then, a well-known medical case had led more Americans to think that abortion laws were too restrictive.

In 1962, Sherri Finkbine of Arizona became pregnant. Finkbine, who already had four children, took some medicine during the early weeks of her pregnancy. She then learned that the drug, thalidomide, increased the risk that her fetus would develop into a deformed baby. Rather than complete her pregnancy, Finkbine sought an abortion. The committee that reviewed therapeutic exceptions to Arizona's abortion laws gave

Fast Fact

Some religious leaders publicly supported Finkbine's right to have an abortion, and polls showed that 52 percent of American women supported her decision.

her permission to have an abortion. County officials, however, could see that the abortion was not necessary to save Finkbine's life—the only reason for which Arizona law allowed an abortion. The issue ended up in court, and Finkbine's lawyer demanded a quick decision, since delaying an abortion would be risky for her health. In the end, Finkbine's hospital decided not to allow an abortion, and she traveled to Sweden to obtain one. At the time, Sweden allowed abortions under more conditions than the United States did.

Sherri Finkbine gave a face to the abortion debate when the state of Arizona denied her right to have an abortion in 1962. Finkbine traveled to Sweden to terminate the pregnancy because she feared that her baby might be born deformed as the result of a drug she had been prescribed.

Finding Jane Roe

The Finkbine case and the growth of what came to be known as pro-choice organizations made abortion a hotly debated topic. Through the rest of the 1960s, more states began to allow abortions under more conditions. Texas, however, kept its old law that tightly restricted abortions. In 1969, attorneys Linda Coffee and Sarah Weddington decided to challenge the Texas law in court. They needed a woman who would agree to try to obtain an abortion and then sue once she was denied it. The woman also had to accept that the case would not be decided in time for her to actually have the abortion. Norma McCorvey, single and pregnant, agreed to pursue the case. Not wanting to use McCorvey's real name, the lawyers called her "Jane Roe" in their legal documents.

Roe and her lawyers sued Dallas County. Henry Wade was the county's chief attorney, so his name appeared on the case as it worked its way through the courts. First, a panel of judges ruled that the case could be heard in a federal court, even though the lawyers were challenging a state law. The judges said that Roe's rights under the Constitution were at stake, meaning that federal courts should be involved. They also said that the Texas law violated a woman's right to choose an abortion. However, the court was not willing to force Texas to stop arresting people involved with illegal abortion. Roe's lawyers then appealed to the Supreme Court, hoping that it would take stronger action.

The Supreme Court began hearing arguments in *Roe v. Wade* in October 1971. The case now included a second abortion suit, *Doe v. Bolton*. After hearing more arguments in 1972, the Court finally reached its decision in January 1973. It ruled that the Texas law was unconstitutional. It then spelled out three basic guidelines for abortion laws: First, abortion was legal in the first three months, or trimester, of a pregnancy. Justice Harry Blackmun, who wrote the Court's decision, said that during this time, the decision to abort "must be left to the medical judgment of the woman's attending physician." Second, states could place limits on abortions during the second trimester. Lastly, states could prohibit abortions completely once a fetus was viable, except if the mother's life was in danger.

> *Fast Fact*
>
> In some legal cases, the people bringing a suit do not want their names to be made public. In other cases, the names of some of the people involved might be unknown. In both situations, men are known as "John Doe" or "Richard Roe" and women are known as "Jane Roe" or "Jane Doe."

TESTING THE LAW

When a person or group deliberately challenges a law, especially to see if it is constitutional, the case is called a test case. Another famous test case besides *Roe v. Wade* was *Plessy v. Ferguson* in 1896. This case challenged the legality of separating African Americans and whites on public trains. The U.S. Supreme Court ruled that the law was allowed under the U.S. Constitution, creating what was called "separate but equal" public spaces for blacks and whites. The Court reversed itself in the 1954 case *Brown v. Board of Education of Topeka, Kansas.*

Famous Figures

NORMA McCORVEY
(1947–)

Norma Nelson McCorvey of Dallas, Texas, married when she was sixteen. She left her husband before her first baby was born and then worked a series of low-paying jobs. By the time she was twenty-two, McCorvey had another child with a different father and became pregnant for a third time. That year, she agreed to become Jane Roe and challenge Texas's abortion law. She eventually had the baby and put it up for adoption. After her famous legal battle, McCorvey did not reveal that she was Jane Roe for many years. In 1995, she became a devout Christian. Her new religious beliefs led her to speak out against a woman's right to have an abortion.

After the Decision

The decision in *Roe v. Wade* struck down or altered existing antiabortion laws in forty-six states. For the first time during the twentieth century, any woman could get a legal abortion during the first trimester anywhere in the country. The decision came as some states were already allowing abortions, but now the legal issue was settled on a national level. The debate, however, was not over. Several groups formed to challenge the *Roe* decision so that all but therapeutic abortions would once again be outlawed. One group, the National Right to Life Committee, had been formed by leaders of the Roman Catholic Church even before the court had made its decision in *Roe*. New groups took a more active role in opposing abortion. Operation Rescue tried to shut down abortion clinics and to prevent women from entering them. Some protesters used violence, bombing abortion clinics, and several doctors who performed abortions were murdered. At the same time, groups who favored legal abortion tried to protect the doctors and fight new legal challenges to abortion.

Those legal challenges began soon after the *Roe* decision and have continued until today. The Supreme Court has ruled that governments at all levels—local, state, and federal—do not have to pay for abortions for poor women who cannot afford them. In addition, personnel at medical clinics that receive federal money can be prevented from talking to pregnant women about how to get abortions. The court has also upheld various state laws that require a waiting period between the time that a woman first seeks an abortion and the time that she actually receives one. Antiabortion (or pro-life) forces believe that during this waiting period, a woman might change her mind about ending her pregnancy.

On the other side, the court also upheld some laws designed to limit protests outside of abortion clinics. Still, Americans who supported abortion rights fought a growing political effort to overturn *Roe v. Wade*.

The Arguments for
Abortion Rights

During the 1960s and early 1970s, Roe's lawyers and others attacked abortion laws on several grounds. Having an abortion, they argued, was a private issue that should be decided by a pregnant woman, her family, and her doctor. Abortion laws took away a woman's right to control her own body. During the 1960s, American women demanded that they receive the same legal rights as men. Such issues as birth control and abortion were part of a growing movement that helped women gain control over all parts of their lives, instead of having to submit to legal and medical decisions about abortion made by men. Some men also saw that the situation was unfair. Richard Lamm, a Colorado politician and future governor of the state, wrote in 1967 that "the right to control her [ability to have children] is a right every woman should have."

A group of female lawyers noted that pregnancy was a unique medical experience, since only women went through it. Laws at the time prevented pregnant women from holding certain jobs, such as teaching and nursing positions. Teenagers who became pregnant could be forced out of schools. An unwanted pregnancy created problems for women that men would never face.

Most doctors who favored changing abortion laws saw a health and safety issue. They knew how dangerous—even deadly—illegal abortions could be when they were performed incorrectly or in unsafe, unsanitary conditions. Giving women access to legal abortions, done by doctors, would reduce this danger. Some doctors also wanted to end the legal problems that they faced if they violated the law in what was basically a medical issue.

In its decision in *Roe v. Wade*, the Supreme Court accepted one of the key legal arguments made against existing abortion laws. Americans, they had earlier ruled, had a right to privacy that was protected under the Constitution. Justice Harry Blackmun, writing for the court, said that "this right of privacy…is broad enough to [include] a woman's decision whether or not to [end] her pregnancy." As noted, however, the court said that this right was not unlimited. After the first trimester, the government had a right to place limits on abortion and consider the health of a viable fetus.

Fast Fact

One of the first pro-choice groups of the 1960s was the National Association for the Reform of Abortion Laws (NARAL), which still exists today.

Fast Fact

The constitutional right to privacy was established in the Supreme Court case *Griswold v. Connecticut* in 1964. This ruling overturned laws that limited a person's right to buy birth control products.

In Their Own Words

Sarah Weddington was one of the lawyers who led the challenge to the Texas abortion law. Here is part of the statement that she made when she argued *Roe v. Wade* in front of the U.S. Supreme Court.

[Pregnancy] disrupts [a woman's] body. It disrupts her education. It disrupts her employment. And it often disrupts her entire family.... Because of the impact on the woman, this certainly, in as far as there are any rights which are [basic], is a matter...of such fundamental and basic concern to the woman involved that she should be allowed to make the choice as to whether to continue or [end] her pregnancy.

In Their Own Words

In *Roe v. Wade*, Byron White was one of just two Supreme Court justices who voted to uphold the Texas abortion law. Here is part of his dissent from the Court's decision.

I find nothing in the language or history of the Constitution to support the Court's judgment. The Court simply fashions and announces a new constitutional right for pregnant mothers.... The Court apparently values the convenience of the pregnant mother more than the continued existence and development of the life or potential life that she carries.... In a sensitive area such as this, involving as it does issues over which reasonable men may easily and heatedly differ, I cannot accept the Court's exercise of its clear power of choice by [placing] a constitutional barrier to state efforts to protect human life and by investing mothers and doctors with the constitutionally protected right to exterminate it.

The Arguments
Against Legal Abortion

Although doctors had pushed for the first abortion laws during the nineteenth century, church groups led the fight to preserve them. The Roman Catholic Church was the most outspoken when the Supreme Court heard *Roe v. Wade*. The church teaches that human life begins at conception. (A woman's body produces eggs. An egg can develop into a fetus when sperm from a man enters it. This moment when the sperm and egg unite is called conception.) Under Catholic teaching, all killing is wrong. Aborting a fetus, at any stage of pregnancy, is a

Antiabortion supporters in St. Paul, Minnesota, also marked the thirtieth anniversary of Roe v. Wade by rallying against the Supreme Court's decision.

form of killing. Some Roman Catholics, however, did agree that abortions could be performed if the mother's life was in danger.

Some of the lawyers who argued against abortion rights pointed to science for support. By the early 1970s, doctors had a detailed picture of how a fetus develops. During the first trimester, the fetus begins to develop features, such as hands and eyes, that make it look like a human. But the lawyers claimed that science had shown that the fetus was alive at conception. The lawyers called the fetus, even when it was only 0.25 inches (0.64 centimeters) long, "an unborn child." The state, the lawyers said, had a duty to protect the safety of this unborn human. Doctors also had to consider the unborn baby a patient and work to protect it.

The lawyers also denied that a woman's right to privacy covered having an abortion. Preventing a conception was much different from killing a fetus. The state could deny people's right to privacy if they committed acts—such as murder—that were clearly against the law.

The abortion debate has continued to focus on when a fetus is truly a human with legal rights, such as the right to life. Some pro-life supporters have accepted that abortion should be allowed if a woman becomes pregnant after a man has forced her to have sex. Some also accept the therapeutic exception. The most vocal pro-lifers, however, believe that abortion should not be allowed under any conditions.

> *Fast Fact*
>
> Many doctors at the time of *Roe v. Wade* rejected the idea that a developing fetus, especially at conception, should be compared to a viable fetus or fully developed baby. Some still reject it.

CHAPTER SIX

The Equal Rights Amendment

WHAT

*Congress passes an amendment giving women equal rights,
but the states reject it.*

ISSUE

The treatment of women in American society

WHERE

Nationwide

WHEN

1972–1982

*D*uring the 1840s, a small group of American women began a movement to win greater social and legal rights for women in the United States. This women's movement achieved its greatest success in 1920, with the approval of the Nineteenth Amendment to the U.S. Constitution. The amendment gave women across the country the right to vote.

In 1920, Alice Paul, a vocal supporter of women's rights, sews the thirty-sixth and final star on a banner, the number of states needed to ratify the Nineteenth Amendment.

To many women, however, that legal victory was just the first step in protecting the rights of women. In 1922, Alice Paul wrote a proposed amendment to the Constitution that would give women equal rights with men. Paul had been one of the most vocal supporters of the Nineteenth Amendment, and she hoped to have the same success with this new Equal Rights Amendment (ERA). Paul and other leaders of the women's movement were trying to change state laws to give women equal rights, and they wanted a stronger guarantee of those rights. Paul said, "We shall not be safe until the principle of equal rights is written in the framework of our Government."

In 1923, Congress considered the amendment that Paul wrote. Under the Constitution, both the House of Representatives and the Senate must approve a new amendment by a two-thirds vote. Then three-quarters of the states must ratify, or approve, the amendment. Paul's amendment, however, did not come to a vote in either house of Congress until 1946. That year, the Senate voted thirty-eight to thirty-five to accept the ERA— short of the two-thirds needed to win.

The Second Women's Movement

Each year, supporters of the ERA continued to submit the amendment for Congress to consider. Each year, it failed to win enough support. By the 1960s, however, many women were becoming more active in politics. They began to challenge old attitudes that women should focus on raising children and taking care of their homes, not on finding jobs. Most women who did work received less money than men did, and they risked losing their jobs if they became pregnant. More women began to talk about the discrimination that they experienced simply because they were women.

> *Fast Fact*
>
> Before the Nineteenth Amendment, only women in several western states had the right to vote, granted under state law.

More women also wanted to change attitudes about sex. Many men acted as if women existed only for sexual relations and as if men could touch women or taunt them about sex without punishment. Women wanted it to be illegal to harass women this way. They also wanted more control over their bodies. Women began to challenge laws that limited birth control, which prevented pregnancies, and abortions, which ended them.

These renewed calls for sexual and political rights marked what has been called the second women's movement. The movement's actions and ideas were called feminism, and its most vocal supporters were called feminists. The early feminist leaders included Betty Friedan, who in 1963 wrote a book called *The Feminine Mystique*. Friedan said that society tried to force all women to be feminine, or "ladylike," and to become mothers and housewives. Young women were taught that they could only truly be women if they played that role, so they should not compete with men, especially in politics or the workplace. This "feminine mystique," Friedan argued, made many women unhappy and denied that they had the same talents as men. In

1966, Friedan and several other women formed the National Organization for Women (NOW). One of its primary goals was to win approval of the ERA.

Famous Figures

BETTY FRIEDAN
(1921–)

Betty Friedan studied psychology and worked as a journalist before getting married and starting a family. During the late 1950s, she began questioning college-educated women about their lives. Friedan found that many of these women were unhappy with giving up careers to focus on raising children and taking care of their husbands. That research became the basis of Friedan's book *The Feminine Mystique*. That book and Friedan's work with NOW led to her being called the founder of the second women's movement. After leaving NOW, Friedan continued to write and talk about women's issues.

Trying to Pass the ERA

During the 1960s, many Americans sought changes in U.S. politics and society. Both African Americans and whites called for civil rights for blacks, and other minority groups sought similar rights. Young Americans protested the Vietnam War (1964–1975), believing that the United States should not be involved in the war and that U.S. leaders had sometimes lied about their actions during the war. Feminism and the women's movement were part of this larger call for greater equality and fairness in America.

By the early 1970s, NOW and American feminists had more supporters in Congress than ever before. In 1971, the House of Representatives voted for the ERA, 354 to 23. The next March, the Senate approved the same version of the amendment in an eighty-four to eight vote. The amendment's supporters included President Richard Nixon, who wrote, "I have not altered my belief that equal rights for women warrant a constitutional guarantee."

Congress set a time limit of seven years for the states to ratify the ERA. Within one year, thirty states approved it—the amendment's supporters needed just eight more states to ratify by 1979. As the deadline drew closer, however, the number of states to ratify stalled at thirty-five. Several states also voted to rescind, or take back, their approval. The opposition to the ERA was strongest in the South and West.

In 1978, NOW announced two new strategies to win ratification. The organization called for a boycott of states that rejected the amendment. NOW asked people and groups that backed the ERA to stop doing business in or visiting those states. The boycott would result in less money going to businesses in those states. The feminists hoped that this economic pressure would convince the states' lawmakers to vote for the ERA. NOW also asked Congress to extend the time limit for ratification. Congress agreed, and in 1979, it voted to give the states three more years to ratify.

Throughout this period, national opinion polls showed that most Americans favored the ERA. The amendment's opponents, however, had become more vocal. To defeat the amendment, they did not have to convince a majority of Americans to oppose it. They only had to convince a handful of lawmakers in several key states that the ERA was not necessary. When the extension ran out in 1982, the opponents had achieved their goal. No additional states had ratified the amendment since 1977. The ERA did not become part of the Constitution.

THE WORDING OF THE ERA

Here is the proposed Equal Rights Amendment approved by Congress in 1972.

SECTION 1. Equality of Rights under the law shall not be denied or abridged by the United States or any state on account of sex.

SECTION 2. The Congress shall have the power to enforce, by appropriate legislation, the provisions of this article.

SECTION 3. This amendment shall take effect two years after the date of ratification.

An information table at the fledgling National Organization for Women's (NOW) fourth annual conference in Chicago in March 1970. The organization, founded in 1966, currently has 500,000 members.

Later Efforts

Almost immediately, NOW and its supporters in Congress introduced the ERA again. During every session of Congress since 1982, national lawmakers have considered the ERA, but the amendment has never been approved. In some states, supporters have tried to convince lawmakers to ratify the original amendment. Feminists argue that the original ratifications in the thirty-five states are still valid and that only three more states need to ratify in order to add the ERA to the Constitution. This move, however, would require Congress to remove the original time restrictions for ratifying.

NOW has also drafted a new amendment concerning equal rights for women. This Constitutional Equality Amendment (CEA) was first proposed in 1995. The CEA includes more detailed language about the rights that should be protected and what kind of sexual discrimination would be outlawed. Congress has not acted on this proposed amendment.

Fast Fact
The last state to approve the ERA was Indiana in 1977.

Fast Fact
The ERA is only the sixth proposed constitutional amendment to be approved by Congress but rejected by the states.

Arguments for the ERA

NOW members and other feminists said that the ERA was necessary to guarantee the rights of women. They believed that old attitudes about women—such as the "feminine mystique"—led to policies and practices that discriminated against women. The supporters also believed that existing laws and amendments that might have protected women were not being properly enforced.

The Fourteenth Amendment to the Constitution said that no person could be deprived of "equal protection of the law." For many years, however, state courts and the Supreme Court said that a woman was not considered a person in legal matters. Not until 1971 did the Court finally rule that women should receive equal protection.

The Supreme Court also limited legal challenges to laws that discriminated based on gender, or sex. In its decisions, the Court had said that governments could discriminate in certain situations, as long as the laws served a clear public interest. However, based on the "equal protection" language of the Fourteenth Amendment, laws could not target groups of people based on traits, or classes, that the Court called "suspect." Race and religion were two suspect classes. In most cases, the Supreme Court would reject laws that discriminated against people because of their racial background or religious beliefs. Feminists argued that gender should also be a suspect class, but the Court refused to accept this.

ERA supporters also had economic reasons for wanting the amendment. They cited figures showing that women had a harder time getting loans than men did. Women also paid more for insurance. Many women also made less money than men for doing the same jobs or ones that required the same skills and experience. In 1982, Representative Patricia Schroeder of Colorado said that the ERA was about survival. "Women have learned," she said, "that equal rights translates into economics."

THE FRONTERIO CASE

As the country was debating the ERA, the Supreme Court decided a case that affected women's rights. In *Fronterio v. Richardson* in 1973, Sharron Fronterio, a member of the U.S. Air Force, challenged a law that automatically gave married men, but not married women, in the military extra pay. Fronterio's lawyers argued that gender should be considered a suspect class under the Fourteenth Amendment and that the law should be declared unconstitutional. On a vote of eight to one, the Court overturned the law, but only four justices agreed that sex should be a suspect class. Since a majority of the justices did not accept that argument, the Court did not have to consider gender to be a suspect class in its future decisions. In general, rulings accepted by a majority of the Court become standards that future justices follow in similar cases.

In Their Own Words

In 1970, Representative Shirley Chisholm of New York was one of only a handful of women—and the only black woman—serving in Congress. She spoke in favor of the ERA. Here is part of her speech.

Discrimination against women, solely on the basis of their sex, is so widespread that it seems to many persons normal, natural and right.... This is what it comes down to: artificial distinctions between persons must be wiped out of the law. Legal discrimination between the sexes is, in almost every instance, founded on outmoded views of society.... It is time to sweep away these relics of the past and set further generations free of them.

Arguments against the ERA

The opponents of the ERA included both men and women. Many were political conservatives who based their arguments on tradition or religious beliefs. Others had economic and legal arguments. Some opposed the feminist movement in general, thinking that it threatened the traditional legal protections that women enjoyed.

In Congress, one of the leading opponents was Senator Sam Ervin Jr. of North Carolina. Ervin argued that existing state and federal laws, along with the Constitution, gave women all the legal protection that they needed. In addition, the ERA was flawed, Ervin and others claimed, because it gave only the federal government the power to prevent discrimination. The critics said that the states should also have a role in enforcing the amendment. Without that role spelled out, the amendment should not pass.

Fast Fact

In 1963, on average, a woman earned fifty-nine cents for each dollar that a man earned.

In 1997, a woman earned seventy-four cents for each dollar that a man earned.

Ervin and others also feared that the amendment would create situations that threatened privacy and could harm women. For example, the critics said, the ERA could lead to legal challenges against separate public restrooms for men and women or separate prisons for male and female criminals. In the workplace, rules that protected women's safety, especially if they were pregnant, would be struck down.

Some critics said that the ERA would allow women on the battlefield or force them to enter the draft—a government process that required young men to serve in the military. Some opponents believed that women should not be actively involved in fighting wars. Ervin said that male soldiers who fought in earlier wars were "opposed to…[subjecting] American girls to similar experiences." He and others also said that the amendment would not let the military remove single female soldiers who became pregnant. The military and motherhood, the opponents said, should not be combined.

Outside of Congress, Phyllis Schlafly led the battle against the ERA. Schlafly ran an organization called STOP ERA. Schlafly and other female opponents stressed that women enjoyed special legal rights or received benefits because of their sex. These women argued that wives and homemakers could lose those rights under the ERA. The amendment, Schlafly said, would force women to pay for half of their family's finances. In a divorce, women often received alimony, a monthly payment from their former husbands. ERA opponents said that women would no longer receive alimony, or in some cases, they would have to pay it to their former husbands. Schlafly said, "[American women] have the most rights and rewards, and the fewest duties.… Why should

Phyllis Schlafly in 1977. The conservative homemaker and attorney spearheaded a nationwide campaign to stop the Equal Rights Amendment.

we lower ourselves to 'Equal Rights' when we already have the status of 'special privilege?'"

Schlafly and her supporters, both men and women, argued that feminists wanted to destroy the American family and the traditional roles of women as mothers and housewives. Schlafly believed that those traditional roles were natural, since only women could get pregnant. Some opponents of the ERA also believed that God had made men and women unequal and that humans should not challenge this arrangement. The feminists, Schlafly argued, were also trying to promote lesbian relations— sexual relations between two women. The ERA would give lesbians the same legal rights as men and women in relationships. Many opponents opposed same-sex relations because of their religious beliefs.

Religious arguments were also used to oppose abortion, which became tied into the fight against the ERA. Because of their religious belief, some Americans said that a fetus, or unborn baby, was a human that deserved full legal protection. To them, abortion under any circumstance was murder. People who opposed abortion said that the ERA would give women the legal right to abortion. In 1973, the U.S. Supreme Court ruled that abortion was legal under certain circumstances. Abortion foes feared that the ERA would make it impossible to limit a woman's right to an abortion in the future. One law professor wrote that the ERA "would make clear beyond any doubt that the states would be disabled from prohibiting or even restricting abortion in any significant way." Schlafly once claimed that ERA stood for "Easy Right to Abortion."

The arguments against the ERA kept it from winning passage before the 1982 deadline. Some similar beliefs have kept it from advancing through Congress since then. Today, fewer women consider themselves feminists, and many believe that existing laws protect their rights.

Famous Figures

PHYLLIS SCHLAFLY

(1924–)

Phyllis Schlafly was already involved in conservative politics in 1972, when she founded STOP ERA (STOP stood for Stop Taking Our Privileges). She wrote articles against the amendment and spoke across the country, launching what she called the "pro-family movement." Schlafly believed that feminists attacked traditional Christian values that stressed the importance of motherhood and the family. Schlafly eventually earned a law degree, wrote more than a dozen books, and founded the Eagle Forum, which promoted a wide range of conservative political issues, including opposing abortion and any new attempts to pass the ERA.

In Their Own Words

In 1972, Congressman John G. Schmitz of California wrote an article attacking the ERA. Here is part of what he wrote.

The amendment would simply dynamite the natural foundation of marriage and our traditional family life. It would [force] married women [into] the same unhappy predicament of unwed and deserted mothers, by lifting from husbands and fathers any special obligation to support their families.... It would also force married women to leave their home and children for work by making them just as responsible for "bringing home the bacon" as their husbands.

CHAPTER SEVEN

The Iran-Contra Affair

WHAT

Members of the U.S. government illegally send arms to
Iran and rebel forces in Nicaragua.

ISSUES

The role of Congress in directing foreign policy;
President Ronald Reagan's involvement in the affair;
the role of politics in driving the investigation
and questioning of the president

WHERE

Nationwide

WHEN

1986–1992

*U*nder the U.S. Constitution, Congress has the power to decide how much money the U.S. government will spend and how it will be spent. This power to determine spending applies to programs at home, defense spending, and aid to foreign nations. With this power to aid other countries, Congress can play a part in shaping foreign policy. The president also has a wide range of powers that influence foreign relations. These include choosing ambassadors to represent the United States abroad, signing treaties, and serving as commander in chief of the military.

During the 1980s, Congress and President Ronald Reagan disagreed on how to carry out U.S. foreign policy in Central America. That disagreement led to one of the largest government scandals in U.S. history. Known as the Iran-Contra affair, the scandal tied together two controversial areas of foreign relations and led to charges that President Reagan might have broken the law.

Crisis in Central America

When President Reagan took office in 1981, the United States was already sending aid to El Salvador. This Central American country was battling rebels who promoted socialism. Many poor Salvadorans supported the rebels, since the government was controlled by wealthy landowners who refused to improve living conditions for the poor. Reagan gave El Salvador more money and military aid, hoping to defeat the rebels.

Reagan saw the conflict in El Salvador and the American role there as part of the Cold War. In this international struggle, the United States competed with the Soviet Union, a communist country with a socialist economy. Each nation tried to weaken the other's interests and promote its own values. Reagan believed that the Soviets, through their allies in Cuba, were trying to bring communisn to El Salvador and neighboring countries.

Events in Nicaragua added to Reagan's fears. A 1979 revolution in that country had ended a pro-American government. The new government was led by rebels called the Sandinistas. They were much more radical than the old leaders and included socialists who saw Cuba as a potential ally. The Sandinistas, however, still wanted political relations with the United States. Reagan believed that the Sandinistas were actually communists, and he cut off all U.S. aid to Nicaragua. After that decision, the Nicaraguan government turned to Cuba and the Soviet Union for more help.

> *Fast Fact*
>
> "Contra" came from the Spanish word for "counter-revolutionary"—a person who seeks to defeat the forces that just won a revolution.

By the end of 1981, Reagan and his advisers had decided to help a new group of rebels in Nicaragua defeat the Sandinistas. The president wanted to prevent the Soviet Union from winning a new friend in Central America. U.S. officials also hoped to stop the Sandinistas from sending arms to the rebels in El Salvador. According to Reagan's plan, the Central Intelligence Agency (CIA), the U.S. government's international spy agency, would train the anti-Sandinista rebels, who were soon known as contras. As required by law, Reagan had to inform Congress that the CIA was about to take action in a foreign country. He did not tell the lawmakers that one of his goals was to overthrow the Sandinista government.

OPENING THE "GATE"

The Iran-Contra affair was sometimes called "Irangate" or "Contragate." The "gate" was a reference to Watergate, a scandal during the presidency of Richard Nixon. In 1972, Nixon and his aides carried out illegal acts related to a break-in at the Watergate office complex in Washington, D.C. The scandal forced Nixon to resign in 1974. After Watergate, reporters often added "gate" to a key word to describe other presidents' scandals or questionable acts. Under President Bill Clinton, for example, possible illegal activities related to the White House travel office were called "Travelgate."

Members of the joint congressional Iran-Contra committee. The investigation of the scandal lasted six years.

Congress Steps In

Some members of Congress did not approve of President Reagan's policies in Central America. U.S. aid in El Salvador was going to military forces that sometimes deliberately killed innocent civilians. The members of Congress also feared that the U.S. government might try to overthrow the Sandinistas or spark a war between Nicaragua and its neighbor, Honduras—a U.S. ally. The contras used Honduras as a base for their operations. Some lawmakers feared that a larger war in Central America would lead the U.S. government to send its own troops into the region.

In December 1982, Congress passed the Boland Amendment. The amendment was part of a law that provided funding for intelligence activities. The amendment said that neither the CIA nor the Defense Department could use any of that funding to aid any group "for the purpose of overthrowing the government of Nicaragua or provoking a military exchange between Nicaragua and Honduras." In private, Reagan told his aides to continue to find ways to help the contras, despite the Boland Amendment.

In 1983 and 1984, CIA employees carried out sabotage in Nicaragua, including blowing up an oil pipeline and placing mines in the country's harbors. Learning about the mines, many lawmakers reacted angrily. Senator Barry Goldwater of Arizona called the mining "an act of war…I don't see how we're going to explain it." Congress then passed a second Boland Amendment that further tightened the restriction on government aid to the contras. Boland II said that no government agency involved in intelligence could use any government funds to help the contras.

Despite Boland II, President Reagan was not ready to stop aiding the contras. He asked the National Security Council (NSC), which had been set up at the start of the Cold War to advise the president on security and defense issues, to find new sources of money for the rebels. One NSC staff member, Lieutenant Colonel Oliver North, led this effort. The CIA and the Defense Department had already turned to other countries to provide aid to the contras. In some cases, the U.S. government offered to give the other countries something that they wanted—such as military aid—in exchange for helping the contras. This kind of arrangement was called a quid pro quo (the Latin phrase means "this for that".)

North worked with both government officials and private citizens who had once belonged to the CIA or other agencies. His job, he later wrote, was to "keep [the contras] alive in the field, to bridge the time between…when we would have no money and the time when Congress would vote again." North's efforts to support the contras in Nicaragua began even before Boland II went into effect.

Fast Fact

The Boland Amendment was named for Edward Boland, a member of the House of Representatives from Massachusetts. Boland led the House committee that reviewed the government's spy activities.

Fast Fact

The countries that gave aid to the contras included Saudi Arabia, which gave $25 million, and China, which provided weapons. Some private U.S. citizens also secretly donated money for the contras.

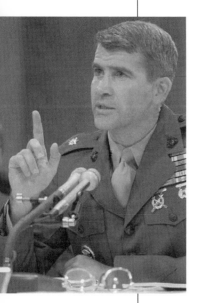

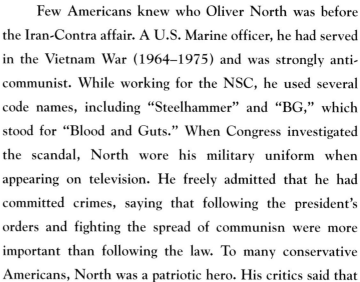

Famous Figures

OLIVER NORTH

(1943–)

Few Americans knew who Oliver North was before the Iran-Contra affair. A U.S. Marine officer, he had served in the Vietnam War (1964–1975) and was strongly anti-communist. While working for the NSC, he used several code names, including "Steelhammer" and "BG," which stood for "Blood and Guts." When Congress investigated the scandal, North wore his military uniform when appearing on television. He freely admitted that he had committed crimes, saying that following the president's orders and fighting the spread of communisn were more important than following the law. To many conservative Americans, North was a patriotic hero. His critics said that he often tried to make himself sound more important than he really was and that his actions made him a criminal. After leaving the military, North began a career as an author and radio talk-show host.

Hostages and Arms in Iran

While trying to help the contras, the United States was also making deals with Iran. Since 1979, that Middle Eastern nation had been ruled by a Muslim religious leader, Ruhollah Khomeini. He and his followers were Islamic fundamentalists: They closely followed the teachings of the Qur'an (Koran), the holy book of the Islamic religion. In November 1979, students loyal to Khomeini had kidnapped more than fifty Americans working in Iran. The fundamentalists kept the Americans hostage until January 20, 1981—the day that Reagan took office. The hostage situation ended what had been strong ties between Iran and the United States.

Under Khomeini, the Iranian government supported other Muslim groups in the Middle East. These groups included terrorists based in Lebanon, a neighbor of Israel, which was the chief U.S. ally in the Middle East. With Iran's approval, the Lebanese terrorists kidnapped several Americans, including a CIA agent. The kidnappings began in 1983. Two years later, Reagan told Americans that he would never make any deals with the terrorists to win the freedom of the hostages. He and others believed that working with the terrorists in any way was wrong. "To do so," he said, "would only invite more terrorism." The United States also refused to sell arms and other goods to Iran, and it asked its allies to refuse also.

Although Reagan said that he would not deal with the terrorists, his administration soon started secret talks with Iran. Reagan and his advisers wanted to free the hostages. They also hoped to develop better relations with some Iranian officials who were not as radical as the fundamentalists. Reagan put Robert McFarlane, head of the NSC, in charge of a plan to secretly sell weapons to Iran, with Israel helping to transfer the arms. In return, Iran said that it would use its influence with the terrorists so that they would release the American hostages. McFarlane and North arranged the deals. At some point, North decided to combine his dealings with the contras and the Iranians. He took some of the profits from the arms sales and used the money to fund the contras.

WAR AND TERROR IN THE MIDDLE EAST

For decades, the Middle East has been filled with violence, and during the 1980s, the troubles there shaped U.S. relations with Iran. In 1983, a terrorist bomb in Beirut, Lebanon, killed 241 U.S. Marines stationed there. U.S. officials knew that Iran was tied to the terrorists involved. At the same time, Iran was fighting a war with its neighbor, Iraq. Needing arms, the Iranians decided to work with two nations that they considered their enemies—the United States and Israel. Both of these countries were willing to work with Iran, even though they distrusted its leaders. However, the United States also aided Iraq at different times during the war.

The Public Learns about Iran-Contra

In October 1986, the Sandinistas shot down a supply plane flown by an American working for the CIA. The pilot talked about the secret U.S. effort to fund the contras and said that it had been going on for several years. Less than a month later, a Lebanese magazine described one of the secret meetings between Robert McFarlane and Iranian officials. Soon, other reports came out about the deals between the United States and Iran.

> *Fast Fact*
>
> Robert McFarlane left the NSC late in 1985 and was replaced by Admiral John Poindexter. McFarlane, however, continued to take part in the arms-for-hostages deal with Iran.

At first, top U.S. officials wanted to deny both situations or at least suggest that the president and his advisers had played a limited role in them. John Poindexter, the new head of the NSC, wrote, "I do not believe that now is the time to give the facts to the public." In his public comments, Reagan made false statements about the Iranian deal and stressed that his administration had not broken any laws. Later, administration officials found out about North's using some of the Iranian arms money to help the contras. Reagan denied knowing anything about this arrangement.

The reports of the Iran-Contra affair led to a series of public investigations. They included one by Congress and another by Lawrence Walsh, a lawyer chosen by the U.S. Justice Department. During the congressional hearings, North admitted that he had destroyed information and lied to Congress about the use of Iranian funds to help the contras. Poindexter said that he had approved the diverting of funds from the arm sales to the contras but that President Reagan did not know about it.

Walsh led hearings in his role as the independent counsel, or lawyer. He brought criminal charges against a dozen people involved in the scandal. He also discovered evidence that Vice President George Bush had not told the truth when he said that he had not been involved in the Iran-Contra affair. In the end,

Walsh was able to prove the guilt of some of the men that he charged with crimes, including North and Poindexter. Later, however, the verdicts against them were overturned.

In his final report, published in 1994, Walsh wrote that he could not prove "beyond a reasonable doubt" that Reagan had known all the details of the Iran-Contra affair or had broken the law. However, the president, Walsh said, had "created the conditions which made possible the crimes committed by others."

THE PARDONS

During the Iran-Contra investigations, George Bush won the presidential election of 1988. While Bush was serving as president, Lawrence Walsh uncovered new evidence against Caspar Weinberger, a high-ranking official. On December 24, 1992, just weeks before he left office, George Bush pardoned Weinberger for any crimes that he might have committed during the Iran-Contra affair. The president also pardoned five people who had already been found guilty of breaking the law during the scandal.

Attacking the President and Iran-Contra

The investigations of the Iran-Contra affair lasted six years. The main public debate over it, however, took place in the first year or so after Americans learned about the arms-for-hostages deal. Reagan's critics inside and outside of Congress raised several points. They believed that the president and his advisers had broken the law by using government officials to get aid to the contras. The second Boland Amendment clearly prevented that kind of effort.

Some lawmakers also saw a larger constitutional issue. By controlling funding, Congress had a role to play in shaping U.S. foreign policy. The Reagan administration had tried to secretly get around that role by seeking

Fast Fact

North and Poindexter received a grant of immunity when they testified before Congress. This meant that anything they said in the hearings could not be used against them in the criminal trials that followed.

private donations and funds from foreign countries. The Constitution deliberately gave Congress control over money issues ("the purse") while giving the president power to handle military affairs ("the sword"). Those two powers were supposed to be separate. The congressional committee that reviewed the scandal wrote that "using funds obtained from outside Congress undermines the [constitutional] Framers' belief that 'the purse and the sword must never be in the same hands.'"

While many Americans believed that President Ronald Reagan lied to the American public about his role in the Iran-Contra affair and disregarded constitutional laws prohibiting actions he took during that time, few people in government believed that the country should suffer through the impeachment process necessary to remove him from office.

Judging from what they knew in 1987, some Americans believed that President Reagan should be impeached, or removed from office for breaking the law. Representative Henry Gonzalez of Texas tried to convince Congress to consider this idea, but few lawmakers agreed with him. A liberal church group, the Unitarian Universalist Association, also called for impeachment. It said that the congressional hearings had shown that the Reagan administration had disregarded "Constitutional processes" and "violated laws passed by the United States Congress."

The work done by Lawrence Walsh proved that the Reagan administration had tried to cover up illegal acts. President Reagan seems to have known about some of those acts or the attempts to hide them. At the least, he and Vice President Bush sometimes lied about what they knew. During the congressional hearings, however, many lawmakers believed that the country did not want to go through an impeachment process. Less than fifteen years before, Congress had started to impeach Richard Nixon for his role in Watergate. According to a newspaper report, one U.S. senator said the lawmakers decided that "the country didn't need another Watergate." That feeling might have kept Congress and the public from an even stronger response to the Iran-Contra affair.

Defending President Reagan

Throughout his presidency, Ronald Reagan promoted conservative values and policies. Many of his supporters believed that Reagan's critics used the Iran-Contra affair as an excuse to attack him and his conservative values. Some of Reagan's defenders also believed that the Boland Amendments unfairly limited the president's ability to conduct foreign policy. If that were true, efforts to get around the limits served a valuable purpose, even if they broke the law. Fawn Hall, an aide to Oliver North, told Congress, "Sometimes you have to go above the written law." Some Americans also believed that the president and his advisers sometimes had to keep secrets from the public.

When Oliver North and John Poindexter spoke to Congress, they clearly took the blame for diverting money to the Iranians. They repeated what Reagan had already said: that he did not know about that deal. "I realized," the president said in August 1987, "I had not been fully informed." To Reagan's defenders, the congressional hearings were meant to somehow find the president guilty of something that he had already said that he did not know about. Republican senator Barry Goldwater wrote, "It became perfectly obvious from the outset that the purpose of the hearings was to get the president." Conservative minister Pat Robertson had a similar view: "The motive for the Iran-Contra hearings was an attempt to weaken a popular Republican president."

In the final report from the congressional hearings, some Republican lawmakers refused to accept the majority's decisions. They also believed that the concern about the affair was based on politics. To these lawmakers, the arms-for-hostages deal and the contra funding were "mistakes in judgment, and nothing more." Reagan's supporters on the committee said that future presidents should have more power to conduct foreign affairs in secret.

In Their Own Words

John Kerry was a U.S. senator during the congressional hearings on Iran-Contra. In 1988, he appeared on *The Secret Government*, a television report on the affair. Here is some of what he said.

I don't think the president of the United States knew these things were going on. But the president of the United States did encourage to such a degree the continuation of aid to the contras, and it was so clear...that this was going to please the president if it happened. It's clear that there were those who turned their heads and looked the other way because they knew that this major goal was out there.... Which larger goal, obviously, was against the law and against the wishes of the Congress and the American people.

In Their Own Words

Here is part of a statement that Oliver North made during his appearance at the congressional hearings on Iran-Contra.

It is mind boggling to me that...some here have attempted to criminalize policy differences between [Congress and the president] and the [president's] conduct of foreign affairs.... I suggest to you that it is the Congress which must accept at least some of the blame in the Nicaraguan freedom fighters matter. Plain and simple, Congress is to blame because of the...unpredictable, on-again, off-again policy toward the...so-called Contras. I do not believe that the support of the [contras] can be treated as the passage of a budget.... The Contras...are people...who have had to support a desperate struggle for liberty with sporadic and confusing support from the United States of America.

CHAPTER EIGHT

Affirmative Action in Public Universities

WHAT

The U.S. Supreme Court decides two cases regarding admission policies at the University of Michigan.

ISSUE

The legality of affirmative action

WHERE

Nationwide

WHEN

2003

*I*n 1954, in the case of *Brown v. Board of Education*, the U.S. Supreme Court ruled that school systems could not segregate, or separate, students based on their race. That decision ended decades of "separate but equal" laws. Many states, mostly in the South, had tried to separate whites and African Americans in public places. The states argued that the buildings and services for both races were equal, but in reality, blacks usually did not receive the same treatment as whites.

Despite the ruling in *Brown*, African Americans still faced discrimination and segregation. Starting in 1961, the U.S. government tried to ensure that blacks received equal treatment in all areas of public life. That year, President John F. Kennedy issued an order that called for more diversity among government employees. This meant hiring more people from minority groups, such as African Americans and Hispanics. Companies that worked for the government were also expected to diversify. They were expected to "take affirmative action to ensure that applicants are employed and treated fairly." The term "affirmative action" was soon used to describe any program or policy that promoted diversity and gave minorities an advantage in such things as hiring, finding housing, or entering colleges.

Fast Fact

The Civil Rights Act of 1964 strengthened the U.S. government's commitment to end discrimination. One part of the law, Title VI, forbids discrimination in any program or activity that receives federal funds.

The push for affirmative action affected many public universities. The schools set up programs to boost the number of minority students that enrolled. For example, in 1970, the University of California at Davis (UCD) introduced an affirmative action program in its medical school. Out of 100 openings each year for new students, the college set aside sixteen positions for minorities. The program meant that some white students with higher grades than the minority students might be kept out of the school.

Affirmative Action in the Courts

Twice during the early 1970s, Allan Bakke applied to the medical school at UCD. He was rejected both times. In 1974, he sued the school, claiming that the program for minority students—sometimes called a quota or set-aside—was illegal. Under the 1964 Civil Rights Act, public schools were not allowed to discriminate based on race. The law was meant to protect minorities, but Bakke said that he was being denied his legal rights because of his race—he was white. He could not get into the special program, and students who did enter the school that way sometimes had lower test scores and grades than white students. Bakke's lawyer argued that the affirmative action program at UCD violated the "equal protection" clause of the Fourteenth Amendment of the U.S. Constitution. This part of the amendment says that all laws must treat citizens equally.

In 1977, the U.S. Supreme Court heard Bakke's case (*Regents of the University of California v. Bakke*). Its final decision was one of the most complicated ever made by the Court. The justices basically split into two separate groups as they decided two main issues. The first was whether the University of California quota system

Demonstrators at the federal courthouse in New York City in 1978 protest the U.S. Supreme Court's decision that Allan Bakke was a victim of reverse discrimination.

discriminated against Bakke. The second—as described by Justice Lewis Powell—was, "Is it ever permissible to consider race as a factor relevant to the admission of applicants to a university?"

The Court ruled that the quota system was illegal and that Bakke should be admitted. In general, all quotas were illegal, unless they were meant to address past discrimination based on race. The university, however, did not have a history of intentional racial discrimination. In this case, Bakke had been the victim of reverse discrimination.

On the second point, the Court said that race could be one factor that the school used to choose its students. Schools had the right to promote diversity within their classes. This ruling meant that the University of California could use affirmative action programs as long as they did not include quotas.

The *Bakke* decision on quotas dealt specifically with public schools, but the law behind it applied to any public organization that received federal money. In a later decision, the Supreme Court denied claims of reverse discrimination when private organizations set up quotas. The Court also later asserted that quotas in public organizations were legal when they tried to correct past cases of discrimination. In some cases, affirmative action programs were set up for women, and the Court also supported these.

Fast Fact

Affirmative action programs that have the effect of limiting opportunities for whites lead to what is sometimes called "reverse discrimination."

Although the Supreme Court generally backed affirmative action, many whites—and some African Americans—continued to argue that it was unfair. Critics said that equality in the United States was about having an equal chance to succeed. It did not mean that everyone would always achieve the same result. Reverse discrimination, critics said, was as unfair as the discrimination against minorities that had occurred before the government and other organizations started affirmative action programs.

Famous Figures

ALLAN BAKKE
(1940–)

Allan Bakke was thirty-two the first time that he applied to the UCD medical school. Previously, he had earned a college degree in engineering and served in the U.S. Marine Corps. Bakke's age worked against him; most medical schools prefer to take new students in their early or mid-twenties. Still, he had good grades and test scores. In his legal battle, Bakke and his lawyer did not argue that the school should admit him because of his excellent school record—even though it was better than the results from the accepted minority students. Instead, they focused on the unfairness of the affirmative action program. The Supreme Court's decision in the case led to Bakke's attending UCD and earning a medical degree.

The Michigan Cases

Starting in the 1980s, some conservative Americans again challenged affirmative action. A group called the Center for Individual Rights (CIR), founded in 1988, focuses on legal issues that limit individual freedom or rights. In 1997, it began working on two cases involving affirmative action at the University of Michigan. The cases eventually reached the Supreme Court, and the media focused more attention on them than on any other affirmative action cases since *Bakke*. Critics of affirmative action hoped that the Court would finally end the legal protection for affirmative action programs. Supporters feared that the United States would weaken its commitment to racial equality if the Supreme Court ruled against affirmative action in public universities.

In one of the Michigan cases, two white students, Jennifer Gratz and Patrick Hamacher, challenged the admittance policy at the university's undergraduate school. This school offers classes in

The Supreme Court decision on affirmative action policies at the University of Michigan focused more attention on the issue than at any time since the Bakke decision. Students Patrick Hamacher, Jennifer Gratz, and Barbara Grutter charged the university in two separate cases that resulted in two separate outcomes.

such subjects as history, English, and biology to students with a high school education. The students and the CIR argued that the school's affirmative action program unfairly kept out qualified white students while admitting minorities who were not qualified. As Bakke did during the 1970s, Gratz and Hamacher claimed that the system was illegal under the Civil Rights Act of 1964 and the equal protection clause of the Fourteenth Amendment.

In a television interview in 2000, Jennifer Gratz said, "I think that the policy needs to be changed. I don't think that there was a fair process." The district court that first heard the case agreed with her. The court ruled that the admission system used when Gratz applied created an illegal quota for minorities. (After 1998, the school used a new system, which the court said was legal.) The University of Michigan then appealed the decision to the Sixth Circuit Court, but the Supreme Court agreed to step in before the circuit court ruled. The Supreme Court decided to hear *Gratz v. Bollinger* at the same time that it heard the second Michigan case, *Grutter v. Bollinger.* (Lee Bollinger was president of the university.)

Barbara Grutter had applied for admission to the University of Michigan Law School. Her application was rejected. She also claimed that the application system used reverse discrimination to keep out qualified whites—like her—while accepting minorities with lower test scores and grades. The district court said that using race as part of the admission process was illegal. In May 2002, the Sixth Circuit Court overturned that decision, saying that race could be used as one factor and that the university's affirmative action program in the law school was not a quota.

The Supreme Court Decides

Early in 2003, the Supreme Court began hearing arguments in the two Michigan cases. The U.S. government supported Gratz and Grutter. President George W. Bush said that the school was trying to do something good by helping minorities, but that the affirmative action program's "result is discrimination, and that discrimination is wrong." The new president of the University of Michigan, Mary Sue Coleman, had this response: "We believe the Court will reaffirm its decision in *Bakke* and find that the University of Michigan's admissions system is fair and legal under the Constitution."

In June 2003, the Court announced its decisions. In *Gratz v. Bollinger*, it ruled that the affirmative action system in place at the time that Gratz applied was illegal. The program used a point system to decide if a student could enroll at the school; successful applicants needed 100 points. Minority applicants automatically received twenty points for being members of a minority group. The Court ruled that the system was not "narrowly tailored" enough to be made constitutional.

In *Grutter v. Bollinger*, the Court found that the law school's affirmative action program was legal. Applicants were not judged on a point system, and race was just one factor that the school considered. The Court said that this system was narrowly tailored enough and met all the standards set by Justice Lewis Powell in *Bakke* for a legal affirmative action program.

Fast Fact

At the end of the 1960s, only 211 African American students across the United States attended medical schools at universities that had a majority of white students.

FRIENDS OF THE COURT

In important Supreme Court cases, many people and organizations might have an interest in the issues at stake. These groups can file legal documents called amicus curiae briefs, which are meant to persuade the court to agree with a particular argument. (*Amicus curiae* is Latin for "friend of the court.") In the University of Michigan cases, seventy-five people and groups filed amicus curiae briefs supporting the school. These included important businesses, such as IBM, and a group of former U.S. military officers.

In Support of Affirmative Action

In the *Bakke* case, Justice Powell defined several points for deciding if an affirmative action program at a public school was legal. A person's race could be only one of several factors considered, and race could be used only to achieve diversity. Having diversity in public schools, Powell said, served a "compelling state interest." In the Michigan cases, the school and its supporters argued that its affirmative action programs met those standards.

Patricia Gurin, a professor at the University of Michigan, issued a report that outlined the importance of racial and ethnic diversity at a university. She based her thinking on a number of studies done at colleges across the United States. Gurin said that attending a school with people of all backgrounds prepared students for American society, which is racially and ethnically diverse. Students also benefited from hearing the ideas and learning about the lifestyles of people different from them. This exchange of differing views "enables students to get to know one another and appreciate both similarities and differences."

Another educator who spoke for the school was Derek Bok. A lawyer, Bok had served as the president of Harvard University in Massachusetts. Bok said that racial and ethnic diversity improved the education that a school offered. Not all learning takes place in the classroom, he said; students learn outside of class as well. Bok argued that students learn more when they interact with classmates of different backgrounds. "Diversity," he argued, "is a benefit for all students, minorities and nonminorities alike."

Many of the amicus curiae briefs also argued for the benefits of diversity in higher education. Justice Sandra Day O'Connor noted this in her decision for the Supreme Court. She cited arguments that said a diverse, well-educated workforce helps U.S. companies compete around the world. She also quoted military leaders who said that a "highly qualified, racially diverse officer corps...is essential to the military's ability to fulfill its principal mission to provide national security."

Other supporters of the University of Michigan focused on fairness and equality, rather than legal points. They argued that the United States still had not achieved true racial justice, despite civil rights laws and the protection offered under the Fourteenth Amendment. As Justice Ruth Bader Ginsburg noted in *Gratz v. Bollinger*, "The stain of generations of racial oppression is still visible in our society." One African American student who benefited from

In Detroit in March 2003, hundreds of demonstrators gather to support affirmative action and the University of Michigan's admissions policies before the U.S. Supreme Court's decision on their legality.

Michigan's affirmative action program said that he lacked the grades to get in on his own. His family was poor and moved often, which might have kept him from doing well in high school. However, once he entered the university, he excelled. "I probably wouldn't have been accepted…had there not been affirmative action."

In Their Own Words

Gerald Ford, who served as U.S. president from 1974 to 1977, graduated from the University of Michigan. He supported the school and opposed efforts to end its affirmative action programs. Here is part of an article that he wrote in 1999 for the *New York Times*.

At its core, affirmative action should try to offset past injustices by [creating] a campus population more truly reflective of modern America and our hopes for the future…. It is estimated that by 2030, 40 percent of all Americans will belong to various racial minorities…. I don't want future college students to suffer the cultural and social [loss] that afflicted my generation…. Do we really want to risk turning back the clock to an era when [minorities] were isolated and penalized for the color of their skin, their economic standing, or national ancestry?

Arguments against Affirmative Action

Despite the Supreme Court's ruling in *Bakke*, opponents of affirmative action believed that it was unconstitutional discrimination. Some of the critics attacked specific parts of Michigan's admission system, while others argued against Justice Powell's decision in *Bakke*. Some also attacked the racist attitudes that they saw in affirmative actions programs.

To Gratz and Grutter, the law was clear: Discrimination against whites, based on their race, was as bad—and as illegal—as discrimination against African Americans. One of their lawyers from the CIR said that "public universities have no right under the Equal Protection Clause [of the Fourteenth Amendment] to engineer a particular racial mix of students." Even if the *Bakke* decision were right—which the CIR did not accept—the Michigan program had several flaws. In both the law school and the undergraduate liberal arts school, the affirmative action programs were actually quotas, which were illegal.

Several Supreme Court justices agreed with some of the CIR's arguments, and they dissented from the Court's decision. Chief Justice William Rehnquist faulted a legal doctrine that the majority of the justices used, called "strict scrutiny." The Court closely studies whether a law that might conflict with the equal protection clause serves a "compelling state interest." In other words, some unequal treatment could be allowed if it served a higher legal goal. Rehnquist and several other justices agreed that the reverse discrimination that occurred under Michigan's affirmative action programs did not meet the strict scrutiny standards. Part of the problem, the chief justice wrote, was that the school did not set a time limit for ending its affirmative action program.

Justice Antonin Scalia agreed with part of the majority's decision, but he also dissented from other parts of it. He wrote that the Constitution clearly did not allow affirmative action, because it prohibited "government discrimination on the basis of race, and state-provided education is no exception."

Fast Fact

In 1996, California voters decided to change the state's constitution to forbid affirmative action programs in any government agency. Therefore, the Supreme Court's decision in the Michigan cases did not affect public universities in California.

Justice Clarence Thomas agreed with most of what Scalia and Rehnquist wrote, and he also wrote his own statement. Thomas was the only African American justice on the court. Like earlier critics of affirmative action, he argued that affirmative action programs were based on the racist belief of some whites that blacks needed special help because they lacked the skills to succeed on their own. The programs hurt some blacks in the long run because they began to expect special treatment, rather than working hard to achieve their goals. Thomas wrote, "I believe blacks can achieve in every avenue of American life without the meddling of university [programs]." Thomas and others believed that discrimination based on race is always wrong, no matter who benefits.

In Their Own Words

Here is part of the brief filed by Barbara Grutter's lawyers when they appeared before the U.S. Supreme Court.

No value is more central to the principles of the Nation's founding than the one that was incorporated into the Constitution through the Equal Protection Clause of the Fourteenth Amendment, the "core purpose" of which is "to do away with all governmentally imposed discrimination based on race."... To be sure, the solemn promise of equality held out by the Fourteenth Amendment is one that has not always been honored. But just as assuredly, there is today a consensus that the Nation's greatness can be measured in substantial part by the steps it has taken towards enforcing the promise of equality, while the [worst] episodes and eras in our history are just so precisely because they mark denials of that promise.... The Law School's use of race and ethnicity to classify and prefer individuals one over another based on those characteristics is a fundamental departure from the guarantee of governmental nondiscrimination.

CHAPTER NINE

The Impeachment of Bill Clinton

WHAT
The U.S. House of Representatives
impeaches President Bill Clinton on two charges,
but the Senate finds him innocent.

ISSUE
Which presidential actions call for impeachment

WHERE
Nationwide

WHEN
1998–1999

*W*hen Governor Bill Clinton of Arkansas first ran for president in 1992, some people questioned his past behavior. Clinton, a Democrat, admitted that he had once been involved with another woman while married to his wife, Hillary Rodham Clinton. Rumors also spread that he had seen other women while he was married. Other critics attacked Clinton because he had tried to avoid military service during the Vietnam War (1964–1975). Some Americans disliked the fact that he had smoked marijuana, though he claimed that he never actually inhaled the drug. Many Republicans, particularly conservatives, began to call Clinton "Slick Willie," because he often tried to talk himself out of trouble.

Despite his problems, Clinton won the Democratic Party's nomination for the presidency. In November 1992, he defeated President George H.W. Bush, a Republican, and business owner Ross Perot, who had formed his own party. Clinton's critics continued to claim that he lacked the morality to be a good president, and Clinton soon faced several scandals. In each case, however, the Republicans could not prove that Clinton had broken any laws, and he remained popular with many Americans. In 1996, he easily won reelection.

> *Fast Fact*
>
> In 1992, Clinton won the presidency with just 43 percent of the popular vote.

Paula Jones and Whitewater

Two of President Clinton's scandals rose out of his service as governor of Arkansas. In 1994, the U.S. Justice Department chose attorney Robert Fiske to investigate the Whitewater deal, a land transaction that Clinton and his wife had made in Arkansas. Fiske's title was independent counsel. In that position, he collected evidence on specific charges against government officials. In August, Kenneth Starr took over for Fiske.

Starr had ties to a group of private lawyers pursuing a second case against President Clinton. Paula Jones had worked for the state of Arkansas while Clinton was governor. In 1994, she filed a legal suit claiming that Clinton had made unwanted sexual advances to her in 1991. For three years, the Jones case and the Whitewater investigation went on separately, but late in 1997, they began to merge. Jones's lawyers wanted to question women who had been sexually involved with Clinton. These women included Monica Lewinsky, an intern at the White House. Linda Tripp, a friend of Lewinsky's, had told Jones's lawyers that Lewinsky had described having a sexual affair with President Clinton.

Through Tripp, Starr learned that President Clinton's friend, Vernon Jordan, had tried to arrange a new job for Lewinsky outside of the government. Jordan had done something similar for some of the people involved in Whitewater. In that case, Starr believed, Jordan had tried to help people who might give evidence against Clinton. Jordan's help was supposed to guarantee that they would not testify against the president. Starr thought that Jordan was trying to do the same thing with Lewinsky.

Famous Figures

KENNETH STARR
(1946–)

As a student, Kenneth Starr studied law at North Carolina's Duke University. He served as a private lawyer before entering government service in 1981, taking a job with Republican president Ronald Reagan. Under President Bush, Starr served as the solicitor general—the lawyer who argues cases for the U.S. government in front of the U.S. Supreme Court. As the chief lawyer in the Office of the Independent Counsel, Starr spent almost four years investigating Bill Clinton. The president's defenders questioned Starr's ability to have a truly unbiased opinion, noting his long years of service under Republican presidents. However, his supporters argued that Starr was honest and hardworking and could do his job fairly. Starr currently works for a Washington, D.C., law firm.

The President Speaks—and Lies

In December 1997, President Clinton answered questions submitted by Paula Jones's lawyers. Clinton said that he had never had sexual relations with any government employee. A few weeks later, he specifically denied having had sexual relations with Lewinsky. Clinton also said that he could not remember if he had ever been alone with Lewinsky in his office. Thanks to Tripp's evidence—which came from secretly recorded conversations with Lewinsky—Jones's lawyers and Starr knew that the president was lying.

After giving testimony, Clinton talked to his private secretary, Bettie Currie. She had often seen Lewinsky when the intern had visited the president in his office. Clinton said to Currie, "You were always there when she was there, right?...We were never really alone." Starr later used this and similar comments to accuse the president of trying to encourage Currie and Lewinsky to lie about the nature of Clinton's relationship with his intern. Under oath, however, Lewinsky confirmed her relationship with Clinton in great detail. Then on January 26, 1998, Clinton addressed the nation and said, "I want you to listen to me. I'm going to say this again. I did not have sexual relations with that woman, Miss Lewinsky. I never told anyone to lie, not a single time. Never."

A LEGAL LOSS

As Paula Jones's case progressed, President Clinton resisted speaking about his relationship with Jones under oath. If he took an oath and then lied, he would be breaking the law. Clinton and his lawyers claimed that an acting president did not have to testify, or speak under oath, about his actions before he became president. The trial would have to be delayed until after he left office. In 1997, however, the U.S. Supreme Court ruled that Jones had a right to bring her case against Clinton, and he had to testify.

The Impeachment Begins

Through the spring and summer of 1998, Starr continued to collect evidence against the president. In September, he gave Congress his final report on the Lewinsky scandal. Starr concluded that Clinton had lied under oath—a crime known as perjury. Starr also said that Clinton had tried to obstruct justice, or prevent the truth from coming out during a legal investigation, which is also a crime. The Starr report said that the president "engaged in a pattern of conduct that was inconsistent with his constitutional duty to faithfully execute the laws."

Impeachment is the first step in removing from office an elected official who has committed a crime. Under the U.S. Constitution, a president can be impeached only for treason, taking bribes, or committing what the Constitution calls "high crimes and misdemeanors." Congress has the power to remove a president through impeachment, in which each branch of Congress plays a distinct role. After debate, the House of

President Bill Clinton was forced to hire private attorneys, David Kendall (center) and Charles Ruff (right), in addition to relying on White House counsel Gregory Craig (left), to defend and protect his interests during the investigation of misconduct led by independent counsel Kenneth Starr.

Representatives decides if a president has done something that is impeachable. The Senate then acts like a jury and rules if the president is guilty of the charges made in the House. If so, the president is removed from office. After receiving the Starr report, the House decided to begin the impeachment process with President Clinton.

In November 1998, the House Judiciary Committee, which focuses on judicial, or legal, issues, heard evidence about Clinton's actions in the Jones case and the Lewinsky affair. Republicans outnumbered Democrats on the committee, twenty-one to sixteen, and the Republicans also controlled the House as a whole. After several weeks, the committee approved four separate charges against Clinton, known as articles of impeachment. The articles focused on the president's alleged perjury and obstruction of justice.

On December 19, 1998, the entire House of Representatives voted on the four articles of impeachment and approved two of them. The vote was largely along party lines: almost all the House Republicans supported impeachment, while almost all the Democrats opposed it.

THE FIRST PRESIDENTIAL IMPEACHMENT

Bill Clinton was the second U.S. president to face an impeachment trial in the Senate. Andrew Johnson, in 1868, was the first. Johnson, a Democrat, had angered many Republicans in Congress with his policies during Reconstruction, the period after the Civil War (1861–1865). In 1868, Johnson fired Edwin Stanton, the secretary of war, and the House accused Johnson of breaking a law that prevented the president from replacing members of his cabinet without Senate approval. Johnson was found innocent on the impeachment charges by just one vote. In 1974, President Richard Nixon avoided a possible impeachment trial when he resigned from office. Nixon and his aides had carried out illegal acts related to a break-in at the Watergate office complex in Washington, D.C. Nixon was accused of trying to hide those illegal acts and then lying about his knowledge of them.

The Senate Decides

On January 7, 1999, the U.S. Senate began its trial of President Clinton. Thirteen Republicans from the House of Representatives presented evidence against the president, while a group of private lawyers defended him. As the trial began, public opinion supported Clinton. Andrew Kohut, who worked for a national organization that polled Americans on a variety of subjects, said during a television interview that a majority of Americans still liked Clinton, despite his actions and the legal charges against him. "When we asked people how is he going to be judged [after finishing his term as president], 52 percent say his accomplishments outweigh his failures."

On February 12, the Senate voted on the two articles of impeachment. Under the Constitution, two-thirds of the senators, or sixty-seven, had to vote for impeachment in order to remove Clinton from office. However, only forty-five senators said that Clinton was guilty of committing perjury, and fifty voted that he had obstructed justice. On both votes, all the Democrats voted against impeachment, with ten Republicans joining them on Article I and five voting with them on Article II. After learning that he would be staying in office, Clinton spoke to the nation. He apologized again for his actions and said that he was "grateful for the support and the prayers I have received from millions of Americans over this past year." Clinton went on to finish his second term as president.

President Bill Clinton

Fast Fact

A poll taken during the Senate trial of President Clinton showed that almost two-thirds of Americans thought that he should not be removed from office.

THE LAST ACT

As Bill Clinton was preparing to leave the presidency in January 2001, a new independent counsel, Robert Ray, was deciding whether or not to charge him with committing crimes. Ray chose not to press charges after Clinton agreed to admit that he had lied under oath while president. Clinton also gave up his right to practice law in Arkansas for five years.

The Case for Impeachment

To the Americans who supported impeachment, the issue was clear: President Clinton had broken the law. His lying under oath about his sexual relations and his attempts to convince others to lie for him qualified as "high crimes and misdemeanors." Given the wording of the Constitution, Clinton should have been removed from office for his actions.

The Starr report noted that "the President made and caused to be made false statements to the American people about his relationship with Ms. Lewinsky." By lying and attempting to obstruct justice, Clinton had "abused his constitutional authority." The House Judiciary Committee made similar arguments when it presented the articles of impeachment to the Senate. Representative James Sensenbrenner of Wisconsin was one of the thirteen Republican managers who argued for impeachment in the Senate. He told reporters that he and the other managers were not attacking Clinton because he was a Democrat and they disagreed with his policies. The managers wanted impeachment, Sensenbrenner said, because of their "devotion to the rule of law, and...fear that if the president does not suffer the legal and constitutional consequences of his actions, the impact of allowing the president to stand above the law will be felt for generations to come."

At the end of 1998, William Bennett wrote *The Death of Outrage,*
a book about the Clinton scandals. A conservative Republican, Bennett
had served under Presidents Ronald Reagan and George H.W. Bush.
In his book, Bennett made arguments against Clinton that were used
again during the impeachment. Here is some of what he wrote.

*If there is no consequence to the president's repeated betrayal of public
trust and his abuses of power, it will have a profound impact on our
political and civic culture. Bill Clinton and his defenders are...lowering
the standards of what we expect from our president; and changing for
the worse the way politics is and will be practiced.... [Other presidents]
made mistakes. But at the end of the day, they were men whose character, at least, we could count on.... We have to aim higher, and expect
more, from our presidents and ourselves.*

Defending the President

Clinton's Democratic supporters saw the impeachment as an
attack on their party and a president that many Republicans
disliked. To Clinton's supporters, his impeachment was harmful,
because it divided the nation over an issue that was not a threat to
the country. Clinton's lying and obstruction of justice related to a
private issue—his sexual relations with Monica Lewinsky. The president had not broken the law regarding any government action.

Clinton's attorney, Charles Ruff, voiced this idea that
Clinton's actions did not equal high crimes and misdemeanors
worthy of impeachment. "Impeachment is not a remedy for private
wrongs," Ruff said. "It's a method of removing someone whose
continued presence in office would cause grave danger to the
nation." Ruff quoted the words of former President Gerald Ford, a
Republican, who noted that impeaching a president "[required]

crimes of the magnitude of treason and bribery"—the two crimes specifically mentioned in the Constitution.

Ruff said that even if Clinton's actions were impeachable, the senators had to judge if the evidence against him was "clear and convincing." Throughout the trial, Ruff and Clinton's other attorneys argued that the evidence did not meet that standard. They pointed to evidence that did not support the House managers' claims. For example, attorney David Kendall pointed out that Lewinsky testified that the president did not tell her to lie about their relationship when talking to Paula Jones's lawyers.

In the end, many senators—both Republicans and Democrats—criticized Clinton's actions. However, they shared the view of many Americans, as noted by Senator Richard Durbin, a Democrat from Illinois: "[The people] said the president's personal conduct was wrong but that he should continue as the President of the United States."

In Their Own Words

On January 21, 1999, Democratic senator Dale Bumpers of Arkansas asked the Senate to acquit Clinton. Here is part of his speech.

We're here today because the president suffered a terrible moral lapse...not a breach of the public trust—not a crime against society....

So, colleagues, if you honor the Constitution, you must look at the history of the Constitution and how we got to the impeachment clause. And if you do that, and you do that honestly, according to the oath you took, you cannot...convict him....

The American people are now and for sometime have been asking to be allowed a good night's sleep. They are asking for an end to this nightmare. It is a legitimate request.

CHAPTER TEN

The Election of 2000

WHAT

The U.S. Supreme Court ends Al Gore's legal challenge to the election results in Florida, giving George W. Bush the presidency.

ISSUES

The legality of Florida election procedures; the role of the U.S. Supreme Court in deciding the election

WHERE

Florida

WHEN

2000

The 2000 presidential election featured Vice President Al Gore, a Democrat, against Texas governor George W. Bush, a Republican. Gore had served with President Bill Clinton for eight years before seeking the presidency. Bush was the son of the candidate Clinton had defeated in 1992, President George H.W. Bush.

On the night of Election Day, November 7, the two candidates were locked in a battle to win the electoral votes of a key state, Florida. Bush's brother, Jeb, was the governor there, and the Republicans counted on a victory. During the evening, however, several news reports predicted that Gore would win—that with his earlier victories in other states, Florida would give him the presidency. Such reports may have been a factor in the final election results: They may have kept voters in other time zones from going to the polls because they believed that the election was already decided.

As the night went on, the reports changed, and some experts said that Bush would win more votes in Florida and become the next president. Gore gave a speech conceding the election, or recognizing Bush as the winner. Several hours later, however, he called Bush and told him, "The state of Florida is too close to call." Gore was not conceding, after all. Out of almost 6 million votes in Florida, Bush was ahead by only several thousand. Under Florida law, the votes would have to be recounted to make sure that there had been no errors.

Fast Fact

During his campaign, George W. Bush called himself a "compassionate conservative." To him, this meant that he favored conservative values, but he intended to support programs that assisted people with special needs, such as the poor and the sick. His father had used the same phrase during one of his political races.

TWO OTHER CLOSE RACES

During the 2000 presidential race, Florida was not the only state with close results. In Oregon, Gore defeated Bush by about 7,000 votes, and he took New Mexico by only several hundred votes.

Members of the electoral college in Rhode Island being sworn in by Governor Lincoln Almond before voting inside the Statehouse in the 2000 presidential election. Al Gore won the popular vote in Rhode Island, thus garnering the electoral votes available from that state.

Popular and Electoral Votes

Presidential elections produce two types of results. The popular vote is the total number of votes that a candidate wins in each state and across the country. To win the presidency, however, a candidate must win a majority of a second vote—the electoral vote. Electoral votes are awarded by special electors, who are chosen by the voters in each state. The number of electors matches the total number of representatives and senators that a state sends to Congress. By winning the popular vote in a state, a candidate wins its electoral votes. A candidate needs 270 electoral votes to win the presidency.

On the morning of November 8, Gore and Bush faced a rare situation. Gore clearly had won the popular vote across the country, but he needed Florida's twenty-five electoral votes to win the presidency. Without Florida, the vice president had just 267 votes. Bush also needed Florida's electoral votes to win, as he had 246 electoral votes. Whoever won the vote recount in Florida would be the next U.S. president.

Gore and his supporters claimed that there had been problems with the voting in parts of Florida. The state used several different kinds of voting machines, and some voters had been unsure how to use the machines. Other voters did not clearly mark a vote for president, leading to what was called an under-vote. Some voters seemed to cast more than one vote for president on the same ballot, leading to what was called an overvote. Democrats in several southern Florida counties wanted a recount done manually, or by hand, rather than using the machines that usually counted the votes.

THE NADER FACTOR

In the 2000 election, several other candidates from small political parties ran for president. The most successful of these was Ralph Nader of the Green Party, who won more than 2.8 million votes—including almost 100,000 in Florida. Some political experts suggested that Gore might have won the presidency if Nader had not run, because Nader appealed to Democrats who might have voted for Gore if Nader had not been a candidate.

Battle in the Courts

Around the country, Americans wondered who would be the next president. A few days after the election, a writer for the *Washington Post* noted, "Our political system blew up on Tuesday. No matter who takes office as president in January, the legitimacy of his presidency will be in doubt." On November 11, Bush and the Republicans went to court to stop a manual recount in the southern Florida counties. A machine recount had already been done there, and the Republicans did not see the need for another recount. Officials in those counties also went to court. They argued that Florida secretary of state Katherine Harris should accept their results, even if they did not meet the state deadline for recounts on November 14. Harris was in charge of the voting process in the state, and by law, she had the authority to declare a winner. The recounts went on, and on November 16, Gore asked another Florida court to force Harris to accept the new results. When the judge refused, the Democrats appealed, and the case went to the Florida Supreme Court. That court said that its goal was to "reach the result that reflects the will of the voters, whatever that might be." The court said that Harris must accept recounts until November 26.

On November 26, Harris announced that Bush had officially won in Florida, with his final count just 537 votes higher than Gore's. At the time, some of the counties had not finished their recounts. The vice president's next move was to challenge the official results, claiming that votes in several counties that should have been counted were not, and that some votes were illegal and should not have been counted. At the same time, the U.S. Supreme Court was preparing to hear a legal challenge from Bush. He believed that the Florida Supreme Court had wrongly decided in favor of Gore.

The legal battles continued for several weeks. On December 4, the U.S. Supreme Court said that the Florida Supreme Court had made a mistake and possibly had ignored the state's laws on how electors are chosen. The U.S. court ordered the Florida court to reconsider its decision. On the same day, a Florida circuit court ruled against Gore, saying that he could not prove he would have won, even if all the votes had been legally counted. The next day, Democratic leaders in Florida filed a new suit claiming that Republicans had broken the law when requesting absentee ballots for thousands of voters. The court ruled that the ballot requests may have been done illegally, but the actual ballots were legal and had been fairly counted.

Fast Fact

A voter who lives in a state but cannot be there for an election can cast an absentee ballot. When Florida's absentee ballots were counted on November 18, Bush's lead over Gore increased to 930 votes.

Famous Figures

KATHERINE HARRIS
(1957–)

Few people outside of Florida had heard of Katherine Harris before November 2000. After the presidential election that month, she was one of the most talked-about people in the country. Born in Florida, Harris came from a wealthy family. She studied in Europe and at Harvard University in Massachusetts and worked in business before entering Florida politics. In the 2000 election, she won the respect of Republicans who believed that she fairly carried out Florida's election laws. Democrats, however, thought that she should not have been involved in settling the disputed election since she had helped run George W. Bush's presidential campaign in the state. In 2002, Harris won a seat in the U.S. House of Representatives.

CONNECTIONS TO THE PAST

The 2000 election reminded some historians of an earlier presidential contest that ended with a close vote. In 1876, Democrat Samuel Tilden won the popular vote and was just one vote short of having enough electoral votes to beat Republican Rutherford B. Hayes. In four states—including Florida—the popular votes were close, and each party accused the other of using illegal tactics to influence voters. The four states eventually sent two sets of electoral votes to the U.S. Senate. Congress had to set up a special commission to decide which set should be accepted, the Republican or the Democratic. The commission accepted the Republican votes, giving Hayes the presidency by just one electoral vote.

The Last Days

Gore seemed to score a victory on December 8, when the Florida Supreme Court overturned the circuit court's December 4 decision. In a close vote, four out of seven judges said Miami-Dade County should manually recount some 9,000 ballots that had undervotes. The recounters were supposed to see if the machine counters had not registered these votes for some reason, even though the voters had tried to mark their ballots. The court also awarded Gore several hundred votes that had already been recounted. Bush and his supporters quickly challenged this decision in the U.S. Supreme Court. The Supreme Court stayed, or placed on hold, the Florida court's ruling. This would give the U.S. court time to hear arguments for and against the Florida decision.

After hearing these legal arguments on December 11, the Supreme Court made its ruling the next day. The court's five most conservative judges rejected the Florida Supreme Court's decision. The manual recount could not go on, because the people doing it could not guarantee that they could use the same standards to judge each voter's intent if the ballot was not clearly marked. Two of the judges also said that the recount would violate the U.S. Constitution, which gives the lawmakers in each state the power to decide how electoral votes are awarded.

With the Supreme Court's decision, Vice President Gore stopped his legal challenges to the Florida vote. Gore called Bush to concede and then made a public statement. He said, "Neither [Bush] nor I anticipated this long and difficult road.… Yet it came, and now it has ended, resolved, as it must be resolved, through the honored institutions of our democracy." Bush soon followed with his own statement: "Our nation must rise above a house divided.… Our votes may differ, but not our hopes." Less than one month later, George W. Bush was sworn in as the forty-third president of the United States.

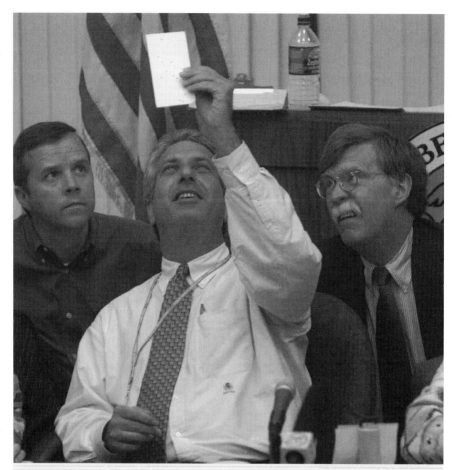

The imprecise nature of some states' voting operations became clear in Florida in 2000 when officials were forced to discount thousands of paper ballots that voters had not marked clearly. In this photograph, Judge Charles Burton of the Palm Beach County canvassing board holds up the last ballot able to be counted while Republican and Democratic lawyers look on.

LANGUAGE OF A RECOUNT

The recount battle in Florida taught Americans several new words and phrases related to the voting process. One of the ballots that was difficult to read and mark was called the butterfly ballot, because its two separate pages suggested a butterfly's wings. A chad is the small area on a paper ballot, usually in the shape of a rectangle, that voters punch out to mark their choices. If the chad was not punched out completely and hung to the ballot by one corner, it was a "hanging chad." A chad attached by two corners was a "swinging chad." A "dimpled chad" was still attached to the ballot, but the voter had pushed on it slightly, creating a bulge or mark. Chads that were hanging, swinging, or dimpled were not counted by the voting machines, leading to undervotes.

The Case for Gore

To Gore and his supporters, illegal actions and unfair vote-counting cost Gore the election. The problem began with the ballots used in some counties. Palm Beach County used the butterfly ballot, and some voters mistakenly thought that they had to punch out a chad on each page. Others did not punch the chad next to the person that they actually wanted to vote for. One voter told the *Miami Herald*, "I came out of the ballot box totally confused."

The Democrats had specific complaints about Republican efforts to keep African Americans from voting. In general, African Americans in Florida tend to vote for Democrats. On Election Day, the Democrats heard reports that some African Americans had gone to the polls only to learn that they were not on the official voter list. Polling officials were often unable to reach supervisors to resolve the problem. In other cases, voters were not allowed to vote even though they reached the polling places before they closed. These and other problems led the U.S. Commission on Civil Rights to investigate the 2000 Florida election. In spring 2001, a majority of the members concluded that "the problems Florida had…were serious and not isolated" and "fell most harshly on the shoulders of black voters."

People who favored Gore also believed that the U.S. Supreme Court should not have played such an important role in deciding the election. Under the Constitution, states are supposed to decide how their electors are chosen. The Florida Supreme Court had examined Florida voting laws, which said that a legal vote "is one in which there is a 'clear indication of the intent of the voter.'" The Florida judges believed that ordering a manual recount to learn the intent of people who turned in undervotes was legal and fair. The U.S. Supreme Court, Gore defenders said, did not have a right to overturn this decision.

In December 2000, it became necessary for the United States Supreme Court to intervene in the legal battle over recounting votes in Florida. The Court ruled that the recount must end due to the subjective nature of Florida officials' attempts to determine the intentions of voters who had not marked their ballots clearly. Upon hearing this decision, Vice President Gore conceded the election to Governor George W. Bush.

In Their Own Words

Supreme Court justice John Paul Stevens was one of the dissenting judges in the case *Bush v. Gore*. Here is part of his opinion in the case.

The Constitution assigned to the States the primary responsibility for determining the manner of selecting the Presidential electors.... Once a state legislature determines to select electors through a popular vote, the right to have one's vote counted is of constitutional stature.... Although we may never know with complete certainty the identity of the winner of this year's Presidential election, the identity of the loser is perfectly clear. It is the Nation's confidence in the judge as a [fair] guardian of the rule of law.

The Case for Bush

Throughout the turmoil after the 2000 election, George Bush and his supporters argued that the recount process was fair and legal. Some Republicans accused Gore of trying to ignore the Constitutional system that had been in place for more than 200 years, simply because he could not accept his defeat. Journalists David Tell and William Kristol believed that Democrats were wrongly arguing that because Gore won the national popular vote, "he somehow deserves Florida's electoral votes—and thus the presidency."

Some Bush supporters noted that the butterfly ballot, which the Democrats said was unfair, had been designed by a Democrat and approved by leaders of both parties in Florida. If voters had trouble using that or other kinds of ballots, the problem was with the voters, not the system. Other experts pointed out that in every election, a certain number of ballots cannot be counted for different reasons, such as undervotes, overvotes, or voting machines that don't work properly. The fact that there had been some voting problems in Florida did not mean that the state's Supreme Court should be involved in deciding the election.

In court, Bush's legal team argued two of the points that the U.S. Supreme Court considered when it reached its final decision. The lawyers pointed to Article II of the Constitution, which says that only state legislatures can decide how the voters will choose presidential electors. The Bush team also relied on a U.S. law that addresses this issue. The law says that if a dispute arises after an election over how electors will be chosen, "the dispute must be resolved…by reference to 'laws enacted *prior to*' election day." The Florida Supreme Court had violated this law and the Constitution with its ruling for Gore. Some people pointed out that the seven judges on that court were appointed by Democrats. Their ties to Democrats might make them unfairly rule in favor of Gore, instead of following the law.

The Bush lawyers also raised the issue of equal protection: that all citizens living under the same law be treated equally. By ordering manual recounts in only some Florida counties, and by

Fast Fact

During the 2000 election, voting officials in Illinois threw out almost 123,000 punch-card ballots that were not marked correctly, with no legal challenges to this action.

counting hanging, swinging, and dimpled chads, the Florida Supreme Court was not giving all the state's voters equal protection. Counting those unclear votes, the lawyers said, would lessen the importance of "the votes of the majority of Floridians who correctly cast their ballots."

In Their Own Words

After the 2000 election, Stuart Taylor Jr., a writer for the weekly paper *The National Journal,* criticized the Florida Supreme Court for its rulings. Here is part of what he wrote.

To be precise, the Florida court's decision...awarded Al Gore several hundred more "votes" than he would have gained from any fair and credible vote-recounting process.... If enough dimples could be found, it appears, the Florida courts would almost immediately have [named] Gore the winner of Florida's electoral votes, and of the presidency.

Glossary

allies—friends and supporters of a person or country

ambassador—a person who represents a government in a foreign country

amendment—a change or addition to a legal document

ballot—paper or device used by voters to record their choices during an election

bill—a proposal for a new law

cabinet—a group of advisers to a leader

civil rights—legal rights relating to political and legal activities, such as the right to vote

conservative—someone who approves of the traditional ways of doing things and does not want to change

corruption—the use of illegal methods to gain money or power

discrimination—the unequal treatment of a person or group based on such traits as race, ethnic background, sex, or religion

dissenting—opposing the beliefs held by a majority

embargo—a legal effort to prevent goods from entering or leaving a country

espionage—spying

immoral—wrong, as defined by religious or legal teachings

integrate—to mix people of different races in a public setting

intern—person, often young, who works for free to learn about a particular career

liberal—someone who supports personal liberty, as well as some government limits on businesses and individual freedoms in order to create greater social and economic equality

moral—correct, as defined by religious or legal teachings

propaganda—information that is designed to shape public opinion

radical—extreme in thoughts or actions, compared to most members of a community

ratify—to formally approve a suggested action

sabotage—secret actions that destroy property

sect—a religious group

Bibliography

BOOKS

Archer, Jules. *Breaking Barriers: The Feminist Revolution from Susan B. Anthony to Margaret Sanger to Betty Friedan.* New York: Viking, 1991.

Durrett, Deanna. *The Abortion Conflict: A Pro/Con Issue.* Berkeley Heights, NJ: Enslow Publishers, 2000.

Johnson, Darv. *The Reagan Years.* San Diego: Lucent Books, 2000.

Sherrow, Victoria. *Joseph McCarthy and the Cold War.* Woodbridge, CT: Blackbirch Press, 1999.

Tushnet, Mark V. *Brown v. Board of Education: The Battle for Integration.* New York: Franklin Watts, 1995.

Willoughby, Douglas. *The Vietnam War.* Chicago: Heinemann Library, 2001.

WEB SITES

The American Experience—Vietnam Online *www.pbs.org/wgbh/amex/vietnam/*

Children of the Camps—The Documentary *www.pbs.org/childofcamp/*

CNN Interactive Special Report—*Roe v. Wade* 25 Years Later *www.cnn.com/SPECIALS/1998/roe.wade/*

PBS Online NewsHour: The Impeachment Trial *http://www.pbs.org/newshour/impeachment/*

The Rise and Fall of Jim Crow *www.pbs.org/wnet/jimcrow/*

Timeline of the Florida Recount *http://www.cnn.com/2000/ALLPOLITICS/stories/12/13/got.here/index.html*

Cumulative Index